Series / Number 07-028

W9-AZY-582

P. Ripoll

NETWORK
ANALYSIS

DAVID KNOKE
JAMES H. KUKLINSKI
Indiana University

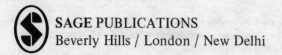

SAGE PUBLICATIONS
Beverly Hills / London / New Delhi

For information address

SAGE Publications, Inc.
275 South Beverly Drive
Beverly Hills, California 90212

SAGE Publications India Pvt. Ltd.
C-236 Defence Colony
New Delhi 110 024, India

SAGE Publications Ltd
28 Banner Street
London EC1Y 8QE, England

International Standard Book Number 0-8039-1914-X

Library of Congress Catalog Card No. L.C. 82-042622

SECOND PRINTING, 1983

When citing a professional paper, please use the proper form. Remember to cite the correct Sage University Paper series title and include the paper number. One of the following formats can be adapted (depending on the style manual used):

(1) IVERSEN, GUDMUND R. and NORPOTH HELMUT (1976) "Analysis of Variance." Sage University Paper series on Quantitative Application in the Social Sciences, 07-001. Beverly Hills and London: Sage Pubns.

OR

(2) Iversen, Gudmund R. and Norpoth, Helmut. 1976. *Analysis of Variance.* Sage University Paper series on Quantitative Applications in the Social Sciences, series no. 07-001. Beverly Hills and London: Sage Pubns.

CONTENTS

Series Editor's Introduction

What is described in this interesting new volume represents a different approach to the world than that of most social science data analysis. As the authors point out in Chapter 2, the social world is most often characterized by the attributes of individuals. But individuals are also characterized by their relationships to one another. It is the study of these relationships that is described in *Network Analysis*.

Networks of relationships between individuals, objects, or events, may be those of friendship, dominance, communications, and so on. The relations may be one-directional or mutual, and they may be characterized by different levels of intensity or involvement. These differences in the content and form of the relationship help define the kind of analysis performed, as explained in the text. In addition, the analysis may be done at several levels, concentrating on individuals and their relationships with specific other individuals or, at the highest level, on the complete network or system of relationships.

Chapter 2 covers the basic terms and concepts that are necessary to understand network analysis. Chapter 3 discusses important points regarding data collection such as the problem of making inferences about networks when what one samples is individuals. Chapter 4 is an introduction to a variety of analytical means of displaying and studying networks. This includes another look at the different levels of analysis, including specification of indices for individual actors, the definition and measurement of cliques, and measures of the equivalence of parts of systems and even entire networks.

While an occasional equation may look forbidding because of double summations and triple subscripts, this monograph requires no more than high school algebra. Moreover, by judicious use of examples, the authors have taken great care to show exactly how the formulas are actually evaluated. With just a little care, the reader should come away from the volume with a good understanding of the scope of network analysis, those aspects of data collection that are important and often overlooked, and the major approaches to the analysis of networks.

—*Richard G. Niemi*
Series Co-Editor

NETWORK ANALYSIS

DAVID KNOKE
JAMES H. KUKLINSKI
Indiana University

They say you are not you except in terms of relation to other people. If there weren't any other people there wouldn't be any you because what you do, which is what you are, only has meaning in relation to other people.

—Robert Penn Warren
All the King's Men

1. INTRODUCTION

Network concepts and methods of social research have undergone dramatic growth during the past decade, particularly in sociology and anthropology. Their rapid introduction to audiences in political science, education, and related fields can be anticipated. A sign that network analysis had come of age was the founding in 1978 of the International

AUTHORS' NOTE: *National Science Foundation grants to both authors and a research scientist development award from the National Institute of Mental Health to Knoke (KP2MH00131) facilitated work on this monograph. Kuklinski gratefully acknowledges his intellectual debt to Heinz Eulau, who has led the way in bringing social relations into the study of politics. Our deepest gratitude to Ronald S. Burt and an anonymous referee for their many useful comments on an earlier draft.*

Network for Social Network Analysis (INSNA) and its two journals, *Connections* and *Social Networks*. A critical mass of active, proselytizing network scholars has formed, and their ideas will percolate through many disciplines as publications and courses presenting these ideas proliferate.

To date, however, few comprehensive basic treatments of networks are available to students and professionals, unlike the vast literature on such traditional statistical techniques as regression, analysis of variance, and log-linear models. Much of the published literature is written by and for insiders who already speak the language of network analysis, leaving interested and curious outsiders to scramble as best they can to decipher the plethora of terms, concepts, and techniques. This monograph is a basic primer designed to guide the interested user through these topics. We systematically inventory the central features of network analysis, cite original sources to be consulted for greater detail, and suggest diverse applications to social scientific research. Our treatment assumes no prior exposure to the subject and presumes no more than a solid background in basic statistics.

The monograph consists of three parts. In Chapter 2, we introduce the idea of relational data and networks, illustrating their application to a variety of substantive topics, units of observation, and types of data. Taking a structural approach, we emphasize the value of network analysis for uncovering the patterns of order underlying empirical observations. In Chapter 3, we devote attention to problems in delineating sets of actors to which network analysis applies, the difficulties in making inferences from samples, the basic requisites for collecting data about relationships, and various special topics in the measurement of ties. In Chapter 4, we discuss both visual (graphic) and matrix representations of some simple networks and various elementary measures of network properties. We present at length various techniques for the quantitative analysis of different types of network data.

Because network analysis is such a broad and rapidly changing methodology, we can do little more in this brief space than provide a general overview. But if we do our task well, we hope that by the end readers will be convinced of the merits of the methods and will continue to pursue advanced topics on their own. If this primer helps to form a foundation that makes such studies possible, we will be well satisfied.

2. BASIC CONCEPTS

Really, universally, relations stop nowhere, and the exquisite
problem of the artist is eternally but to draw, by a geometry of
his own, the circle within which they shall happily *appear* to do so.

—Henry James
Roderick Hudson

This chapter presents concepts essential for understanding network
analysis procedures. Usage among practitioners is not entirely con-
sensual, and we have made no effort to be terminologically exhaustive.
We have, however, attempted to adhere most closely to the labels and
definitions that strike us as belonging in the mainstream of sociological
approaches to network analysis. Throughout, we attempt to illustrate
the basic concepts with citations to recent literature, which the reader
may wish to consult to understand further their application to substantive problems.

To appreciate fully the distinctive theoretical underpinnings of
network approaches to social phenomena, a comparison with more
traditional, individualistic approaches may be useful. In the atomistic
perspectives typically assumed by economics and psychology, individual actors are depicted as making choices and acting without regard
to the behavior of other actors. Whether analyzed as purposive action
based on rational calculations of utility maximization, or as drive-
reduction motivation based on causal antecedents, such individualistic
explanations generally ignore the social contexts within which the
social actor is embedded.

In contrast, network analysis incorporates two significant assumptions about social behavior. Its first essential insight is that any actor
typically participates in a social system involving many other actors,
who are significant reference points in one another's decisions. The
nature of the relationships a given actor has with other system members
thus may affect that focal actor's perceptions, beliefs, and actions. But
network analysis does not stop with an account of the social behavior
of individuals. Its second essential insight lies in the importance of
elucidating the various levels of structure in a social system, where

structure consists of "regularities in the patterns of relations among concrete entities" (White et al., 1976). In the individualistic approach, social structure is seldom an explicit focus of inquiry, to the extent that it is even considered at all. Network analysis, by emphasizing relations that connect the social positions within a system, offers a powerful brush for painting a systematic picture of global social structures and their components. The organization of social relations thus becomes a central concept in analyzing the structural properties of the networks within which individual actors are embedded, and for detecting emergent social phenomena that have no existence at the level of the individual actor. This dualistic quality of network analysis—its capacity to illuminate entire social structures and to comprehend particular elements within the structure—probably accounts for its rapidly increasing popularity among social theorists and researchers who have found the older individualistic tradition wanting as a framework for understanding social phenomena.

Attributes and Relations

Two basic approaches to viewing and classifying the various aspects of the social world—according to their attributes or their relationships—are often treated as antithetical and even irreconcilable. As this monograph must deal at great length with relational data, we need to make clear from the outset how these two approaches to measurement differ. We shall also point out that neither perspective by itself yields satisfactory understandings of social phenomena.

Attributes are intrinsic characteristics of people, objects, or events. When we think of explaining variance among such units of observation, we almost naturally resort to attribute measures, those qualities that inherently belong to a unit apart from its relations with other units or the specific context within which it is observed. Various types of attributes can be measured: an occupation's average income, a nation's gross national product, a riot's duration, a birth cohort's mean formal schooling, a person's opinion about the president.

Persons, objects, and events may also be involved in relationships, that is, actions or qualities that exist only if two or more entities are considered together. A relation is not an intrinsic characteristic of either party taken in isolation, but is an emergent property of the connection or linkage between units of observation. Where attributes persist across the various contexts in which an actor is involved (e.g., a person's age, sex, intelligence, income, and the like remain unchanged whether at home, at work, at church), relations are context specific and alter or disappear upon an actor's removal from interaction with the relevant other parties (e.g., a student/teacher relation does not exist outside a school setting; a marital relation vanishes upon death or divorce of a spouse). A wide variety of relational properties can be measured: the strengths of the friendships among pupils in a classroom, the kinship obligations among family members, the economic exchanges between organizations. A systematic classification of relationships will be presented below.

Many aspects of social behavior can be treated from both the attribute and the relational perspectives, with only a slight alteration of conceptualization. For example, the value of goods that a nation imports in foreign trade each year is an attribute of the nation's economy, but the volume of goods exchanged between each pair of nations measures an exchange relationship. Similarly, while a college student's home state is a personal attribute, a structural relationship between colleges and states could be measured by the proportions of enrolled students coming to each college from each state. We could ask citizens about their attendance at political rallies and thus assign attribute scores for participation, but if we designate sets of citizens who attended the same rallies, we begin to probe their cooccurrence relationships. The point we are stressing is that, while attributes and relationships are conceptually distinct approaches to social research, they should be seen as neither polar nor mutually exclusive measurement options. Undoubtedly, the vast bulk of social research today relies upon attribute measures from surveys, experiments, and field observations of given units of analysis. Relational measures capture emergent properties of social systems that cannot be measured by simply aggregating the attributes of individual members. Furthermore, such emergent properties may significantly affect both system performance and the behavior of network members. For example, the structure of informal friendships and antagonisms in formal work groups can affect both group and individual productivity rates in ways not predictable from such personal attributes as age, experience, intelligence, and the like (Homans, 1950). As another example, the structure of communication among medical practitioners can shape the rate of diffusion of medical innovations in a local community and can determine which physicians are likely to be early or late adopters (Coleman et al., 1966). By ignoring the social-structural context within which actors are located, a purely attribute-based analysis loses much of the explanatory potential that relational analysis can offer. The ultimate advance of social scientific knowledge requires combinations of both types of data and the creation of measurement and analysis methods capable of incorporating them.

Networks

Relations are the building blocks of network analysis. A *network* is generally defined as a specific type of relation linking a defined set of persons, objects, or events (see Mitchell, 1969). Different types of relations identify different networks, even when imposed on the identical set of elements. For example, in a set of employees at a workplace, the advice-giving network is unlikely to be the same as the friendship network or the formal authority network. The set of persons, objects, or events on which a network is defined may be called the *actors* or *nodes*. These elements possess some attribute(s) that identify them as members of the same equivalence class for purposes of determining the network of relations among them. For example, we might stipulate that all payroll employees at plant six of the National Widget Corp. comprise the set of actors among whom an advice-giving network is sought. Additional restrictions on the permissible actors could be imposed (e.g., only males in managerial jobs), indicating that delimiting network boundaries depends to a great extent upon a researcher's purposes.

Our generic definition of a network may imply that only those linkages that actually occur are part of a network. But network analysis must take into account both the relations that occur and those that do not exist among the actors. For example, attending only to the gossip connections in a community and not to the structural "holes" that occur where links are absent might result in an inaccurate understanding of how rumors spread or evaporate. The configuration of present and absent ties among the network actors reveals a specific *network structure*. Structures vary dramatically in form, from the isolated structure in which no actor is connected to any other actor, to the saturated structure in which every actor is directly linked to every other individual. More typical of real networks are various intermediate structures in which some actors are more extensively connected among themselves than are others. A discussion of some basic types of network structures appears below. A core theoretical problem in network analysis is to explain the occurrence of different structures and, at the nodal level, to account for variation in linkages to other actors. The parallel empirical task in network analysis is to detect the presence of such structures in empirical network data.

If network analysis were limited just to a conceptual framework for identifying how a set of actors is linked together, it would not have excited much interest and effort among social researchers. But network analysis contains a further explicit premise of great consequence: *The structure of relations among actors and the location of individual actors in the network have important behavioral, perceptual, and attitudinal consequences both for the individual units and for the system as a whole.* In Mitchell's (1969) felicitous terms, "The patterning of linkages can be used to account for some aspects of behavior of those involved." For example, a formal organization with a centralized structure of authority among its various divisions and departments may be most effective (e.g., enjoying high growth and profitability) in a relatively placid environment, but in a turbulent, rapidly changing environment an organization with a less centralized structure may be more adaptable. Investigating this hypothesis requires a structural analysis of the information collection, processing, dissemination, decision making, and implementation relations linking organizational units. Network analysis offers a means for bridging the gap between macro- and micro-level explanations and it holds out the promise of surpassing if not entirely supplanting attribute-based approaches.

To illustrate the potential power of a network approach, consider a variety of contemporary social science problems: the sources of homophyly of beliefs within a power elite, the adoption of technological innovations, the causes of corporate profitability, the income earnings of occupational groups, the recruitment processes of social movement organizations, the development of nontraditional sex roles. In each of these and many other substantive areas, a large research literature can be uncovered that attempts to explain the phenomena as a function of individual or group attributes. Yet in many instances, such character-istics may predict behavior only because of underlying patterns of relations that are often associated with these attributes. For example, innovation diffusion studies frequently find that highly educated persons tend to adopt sooner, but, this relation may really reflect the tendency for such persons to be more prominent in their networks, thus giving them greater access to the flow of information (e.g., Knoke and Burt, 1982). Network approaches can more faithfully capture the context of social relations within which actors participate and make behavioral decisions.

Research Design Elements

Network analyses take many forms to suit researchers' diverse theoretical and substantive concerns. Four elements of a research design in particular shape the measurement and analysis strategies available to a researcher: the choice of sampling units, the form of relations, the relational content, and the level of data analysis. Varying combinations of these design elements have created a wide diversity among network studies that is evident in the research literature.

SAMPLING UNITS

Before collecting data, a network researcher must decide the most relevant type of social organization and the units within that social form that comprise the network nodes. Ordered in a roughly increasing scale of size and complexity are a half-dozen basic units from which samples may be drawn: individuals, groups (both formal and informal), complex formal organizations, classes and strata, communities, and nation-states. A typical design involves some higher-level system whose network is to be investigated with one or more lower-level units as the nodes, for example, a corporation with its departments and individual employees as the actors, or a city with its firms, bureaus, and voluntary associations as the nodes.

The earliest and still most prevalent network studies select small-scale social organizations—classrooms, offices, gangs, social clubs, schools, villages, and artificially created laboratory groups—and treat their individual members as the nodes (see Moreno, 1934; Homans, 1950; Leinhardt, 1972; Hallinan, 1978; Kandel, 1978; Rogers and Kincaid, 1981; Miller et al., 1981). Although these settings have the considerable advantages of sharply delineated boundaries and enumerated populations, nothing intrinsic to network analysis prevents applications to large-scale systems. Recent examples from the literature include: elite leadership networks in communities (Perrucci and Pilisuk, 1970; Laumann and Pappi, 1976); interorganizational networks in communities (Galaskiewicz, 1979; Knoke and Wood, 1981; Knoke, forthcoming); intercorporate networks in the national economy (Levine, 1972; Sonquist and Koenig, 1975; Burt et al., 1980); scientific networks in a professional discipline (Crane, 1969; Breiger, 1976;

Mullins et al., 1977); and international networks in the world system (Snyder and Kick, 1979).

FORM OF RELATIONS

The relations among actors have both content and form. Content refers to the substantive type of relation represented in the connections (e.g., supervising, helping, gossiping), and an inventory of content types is presented below. *Relational form* refers to properties of the connections between pairs of actors (dyads) that exist independently of specific contents. Two basic aspects of relational form are (a) the intensity or strength of the link between two actors, and (b) the level of joint involvement in the same activities (Burt, 1982: 22). Conceivably, two relations that are quite distinct in content may exhibit identical or highly similar forms. For example, within a small community the social visits between residents might occur with the same frequency and degree of reciprocation as do their exchanges of minor economic assistance (e.g., Hansen, 1981).

RELATIONAL CONTENT

In conjunction with choosing the appropriate sampling units, a network analyst must decide what specific network linkages to investigate. Network content is frequently determined by theoretical considerations; for example, a study of psychological balance theory (Heider, 1946, 1979; Anderson, 1979) calls for sentiment relations. Thus no single type of connection can be a priori designed as *the* correct network for a population, or even the most important network for all research purposes. In some cases, substantive problems indicate that more than one analytically distinct type of relationship should be investigated, in which case a network compounded of two or more types of linkages (i.e., a *multiplex* network) may be most appropriate (Boissevain, 1974; Kapferer, 1969).

Because researchers' capacities to conceptualize and operationalize various types of networks are almost unlimited, we can only list the more common types of relational content, citing some representative studies:

- *Transaction relations:* Actors exchange control over physical or symbolic media, for example, in gift giving or economic sales and purchases (Burt et al., 1980; Laumann et al., 1978).

- *Communication relations:* Linkages between actors are channels by which messages may be transmitted from one actor to another in a system (Marshall, 1971; Lin, 1975; Rogers and Kincaid, 1981).

- *Boundary penetration relations:* The ties between actors consist of constituent subcomponents held in common, for example, corporation boards of directors with overlapping members (Levine, 1972; Allen, 1974; Mariolis, 1975; Sonquist and Koenig, 1975; Burt, 1982: ch. 8).

- *Instrumental relations:* Actors contact one another in efforts to secure valuable goods, services, or information, such as a job, an abortion, political advice, recruitment to a social movement (Granovetter, 1974; Boissevain, 1974).

- *Sentiment relations:* Perhaps the most frequently investigated networks are those in which individuals express their feelings of affection, admiration, deference, loathing, or hostility toward each other (Hunter, 1979; Hallinan, 1974; Sampson, 1969).

- *Authority/power relations:* These networks, usually occurring in complex formal organizations, indicate the rights and obligations of actors to issue and obey commands (White, 1961; Cook and Emerson, 1978; Williamson, 1970; Lincoln and Miller, 1979).

- *Kinship and descent relations:* A special instance of several preceding generic types of networks, these bonds indicate role relationships among family members (Nadel, 1957; Bott, 1955; White, 1963).

LEVELS OF ANALYSIS

After selecting the sampling units and relational content, a network analyst will have several alternative levels at which to analyze the data collected for a project. Appropriate techniques will be described at length in Chapter 3, but here we consider four conceptually distinct levels of analysis at which an investigation can focus.

The simplest level is the *egocentric* network, consisting of each individual node, all others with which it has relations, and the relations among these nodes. If the sample size is N, there are N units of analysis at the ego-centered level. Each actor can be described by the number, the magnitude, and other characteristics of its linkages with the other actors, for example, the proportion of reciprocated linkages or the density of ties among the actors in ego's first "zone" (i.e., the set of actors directly connected to ego). In many ways, an egocentric level of analysis strongly resembles typical attribute-based research, with the usual characteristics supplemented by measures derived from a node's direct network relations. Good examples of ego-centered network research include Laumann's (1973) analysis of friendship among urban men and Granovetter's (1974) investigation of job information transmission.

At the next highest level of analysis is the *dyad*, formed by a pair of nodes. If the sample size is N, there are $(N^2 - N)/2$ distinct units of analysis at the dyadic level. The basic question about a dyad is whether or not a direct tie exists between the two actors, or whether indirect connections might exist via other actors in the system to which they are connected. Typical dyadic analyses seek to explain variation in dyadic relations as a function of joint characteristics of the pair, for example, the degree of similarity of their attribute profiles. Laumann, Verbrugge, and Pappi (1976: 145-161), for instance, measured the proximities among pairs of elites in a German town's community affairs discussion network. Using causal modeling methods, they found values and friendships to mediate most of the effects of party affiliation, religion, formal positions in government, and business/professional similarities on distances between the dyads.

Not surprisingly, the third level of analysis consists of *triads*. If N is the sample size, there are $(\frac{N}{3})$ distinct triads formed by selecting each possible subset of three nodes and their linkages. Research using triads has largely concentrated on the local structure of sentiment ties among individual actors, with a particular concern for determining transitivity relations (i.e., if A chooses B and B chooses C, does A tend to choose C?). Triads received quite elaborate and elegant statistical treatment at the hands of Holland, Leinhardt, and Davis (see Holland and Leinhardt, 1975, 1978; Davis, 1979); we lack the space to review them in this volume.

Beyond the triadic level, the most important level of analysis is that of the *complete network*, or system. In these analyses, a researcher uses the complete information about patterning of ties among all actors to ascertain the existence of distinct positions or roles within the system and to describe the nature of relations among these positions. Although the sample may consist of N nodes and $(N^2 - N)$ possible dyadic ties of a given type, these elements altogether add up to only a single system. Thus to test hypotheses about the causes or consequences of variation in complete network configurations typically requires several distinct systems, which may tax a researcher's resources. Nevertheless, the complete network has become one of the most popular levels of analysis in recent years with the growth of new methods and tools to handle its particular problems. Because the bulk of this book focuses on this type of data, the following section examines concepts useful in analyzing the social structure of complete networks.

This brief overview of four levels of network analysis underscores the important emergence of structural properties that cannot simply be induced from lower-level phenomena. For example, transitivity of choice relations is a substantively important variable in friendship formation theories that can be observed at the triadic but not at the dyadic or egocentric level. As another illustration, consider two scientific research communities with roughly similar egocentric, dyadic, or even triadic structures in their scientific discussion networks. However, if the first community's complete network consists of fragmented subgroups such that many individuals cannot easily reach one another directly or indirectly, while the second community's complete network exhibits a high degree of integration among subgroups, we may well anticipate a freer flow of information and greater innovation in the latter community. This protean capacity of network analysis to address problems at multiple levels of analysis by encompassing emergent structural properties lies behind its increasing popularity as a framework for guiding empirical research.

Structure in Complete Networks

One major use of network analysis in sociology and anthropology has been to uncover the social structure of a total system. Systems may be as small as an elementary school classroom and a native village, or as large as a national industry and the world system of nation-states. But for any system, an important step in a structural analysis to identify the significant positions within a given network of relations that link the system actors. The observable actors—be they pupils, organizations, or national governments—are not the social structure. The regular pattern of relations among the positions composed of concrete actors constitutes the social structure of the system. Hence identification of positions is a necessary but incomplete prelude in complete network analysis, which requires the subsequent appraisal of the relations connecting positions one to another.

Positions, or social roles, are subgroups within a network defined by the pattern of relations (which represent real observable behaviors) that connect the empirical actors to each other. Theorists of social structure, such as Linton (1936) and Nadel (1957), usually reserve the term "status" for a position or role that carries special rights and duties defined by the pattern of relations. All statuses are positions, but not all positions are statuses. By occupying positions in a network structure, individual actors have certain connections to other actors, who in turn also occupy unique structural positions.

Although empirical actors and their observable linkages provide the data for identifying positions, a network's positions are conceptually distinct from any specific incumbents. For example, in a hospital system the positions defined by patterns of relations among actors— given such conventional labels as doctor, patient, nurse, administrator, paraprofessional, and so forth—persist despite frequent changes in the unique individuals occupying these positions. New positions may be created when an actor(s) establishes a unique set of ties to the pre-existing positions, for example, when data processing specialists are hired to manage the diagnostic and administrative information flow of the hospital. The point we are making is that a structural analysis of a complete network seeks to uncover fundamental social positions, as defined by observed relations among social actors. The network analyst's task is to use the network relations to map the empirical actors into the latent positions. In the process, the complexity of the network is typically simplified, reducing a large number of N actors into a smaller number of M positions, since typically several empirical actors occupy the same position (e.g., many doctors, many nurses, many patients, and so on).

In deciding the basis on which to identify the positions in a complete network and to determine which actors jointly occupy each position, the network analyst has two basic alternatives (Burt, 1978). The first criterion is *social cohesion*. Actors are aggregated together into a position to the degree that they are connected directly to each other by cohesive bonds. Positions so identified are called "cliques" if every actor is directly tied to every other actor in the position (i.e., maximal connection), or "social circles" if the analyst permits a less stringent frequency of direct contact, say, for example, that an actor need have direct ties to only 80% of the position members to be included (Alba, 1973; Alba and Kadushin, 1976; Kadushin, 1968). Note that the weaker social cohesion criterion will actually identify multiple positions, for example, leaders and followers.

The second criterion for identifying network positions is *structural equivalence* (Lorrain and White, 1971; White et al., 1976; Sailer, 1978).

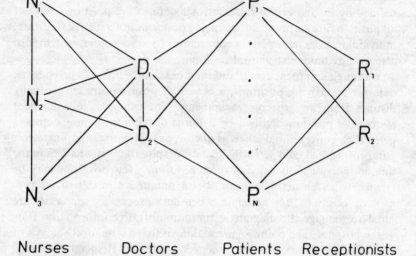

Figure 1   A Hypothetical Medical Practice Network

Actors are aggregated into a jointly occupied position or role to the extent that they have a common set of linkages to the other actors in the system. No requirement is imposed that the actors in a position have direct ties to each other. Thus, a structurally equivalent position may or may not be a clique or circle, whereas a socially cohesive position may contain actors with quite distinct patterns of ties to the other positions.

A simple hypothetical example should make these conceptual distinctions clearer. Figure 1 portrays a fictional medical practice network. The lines connecting the actors represent "frequent contacts on medical matters" (the diagram is an unrealistic representation, but useful for illustrative purposes). A social cohesion criterion identifies two distinct cliques, a small one involving just the two receptionists and a large one containing all three nurses and both physicians. But using structural equivalence criteria, four distinct positions would emerge, corresponding to the four roles labeled in the diagram. Nurses and doctors are no longer aggregated because they differ in their patterns of contacts with the other actors (i.e., the doctors are linked to the patients but the nurses are not, undoubtedly untrue in a real system).

Three of these structurally equivalent positions are also cliques, but the patient position is not a clique because its occupants do not discuss medical matters among themselves. The point of this exercise is that different criteria for identifying structural positions in networks can, and usually do, yield different results. The choice of methods for locating positions in an empirical network ultimately depends, as in the application of any method, on the substantive and theoretical problem the analyst is addressing. For some purposes a clique approach will be preferred, while in other situations a structural equivalence procedure will be more useful. To state a definitive rule about which one to choose that would cover all situations is impossible.

Burt (1978: 209) presents several reasons why the structural equivalence criterion is usually preferred as the basis for identifying structural positions:

> Relative to subgroups based on cohesion, those based on structural equivalence: (1) include a broader range of types of subgroups, (2) extend the scope of types of subgroups in which homogeneity of attitudes and behaviors can be expected, (3) have a more consistent meaning as operationalized by available computer algorithms, (4) can be subjected to statistical tests of goodness-of-fit, (5) are accordingly more robust over random error in relations, and (6) provide a basis for sampling population networks in large systems.

He further argues that cliques can be considered special cases of structurally equivalent positions if an assumption is made of similar types of links to external actors. We shall return to the important concept of network position in Chapter 4 when we discuss methods for detecting cliques and structurally equivalent subgroups in empirical data. Without prejudging the relative importance of the two criteria, we underscore the centrality of the structural position concept to the whole network enterprise.

3. DATA COLLECTION

Amid the seeming confusion of our mysterious world, individuals are so nicely adjusted to a system, and systems to one another, that, by stepping aside for a moment, a man exposes himself to a fearful risk of losing his place forever.

—Nathaniel Hawthorne
Wakefield

In any empirical research, the investigator must attend to two matters: sampling and measurement. Both represent potentially acute problems when the intention is to use network analysis. Boundary specification presents yet a thrid, and unique, problem. Because setting the boundaries is the starting point in the collection of network data, we begin our discussion with this topic.

Boundary Specification

The matter of boundary specification (or "delimiting the graph") can be simply put: Where does one set the limits when collecting data on social networks that in reality may have no obvious limits (Barnes, 1979: 414)? Laumann et al. (1982) presented a cogent discussion of the central issues, organized around a primary dimension of realist versus nominalist views of social phenomena. In a *realist* approach to boundary specification, the network analyst adopts the presumed subjective perceptions of system actors themselves, defining the boundaries of a social entity as the limits that are consciously experienced by all or most of the actors that are members of the entity (e.g., a family, corporation, social movement). In a *nominalist* perspective, network closure is imposed by the researcher's conceptual framework that serves an analytic purpose, for example, defining a social class as all workers having a common relation to a mode of production. The extent to which subjective awareness and analytic imposition produce coincident boundaries is, of course, always an empirical question.

To illustrate the problematic nature of network boundaries, consider the flow of political information among citizens during an election campaign. This is not a new research question: Lazarsfeld and his colleagues (1948) tried to identify social influences on political attitudes in the 1940 presidential campaign. Because they simply asked their randomly chosen respondents to name the people from whom they received political information, they were able to distinguish the personal attributes of "opinion leaders" from "opinion followers," but they could not identify the underlying social structure through which conversation presumably took place (for excellent critiques, see Eulau, 1980; Sheingold, 1973).

Network analysis represents a potentially more powerful strategy for understanding the process by which political ideas move among voters. It entails initially choosing a random sample of citizens and asking them to indicate the persons from whom they receive political information and to whom they give it. (Although network analysis focuses on relations, such linkages cannot be sampled directly, so the usual procedure is to identify the relevant population of actors, draw a sample of actors, and either ask about or directly observe their relations.) "Snowball sampling" outward (Goodman, 1961), the researcher might then interview each of the named persons ("first zone" respondents) as well as those persons the first zone respondents name. But what about third, fourth, and tenth zone persons? Where does a researcher stop? Unfortunately, there is no criterion for deciding how many zones to snowball outward from the original sample. And no matter where the investigator stops, complete enumeration almost certainly will not have been achieved. The decision about where to draw the boundary must ultimately be set by social-theoretic considerations of the phenomenon under investigation. For some problems such as political information a two-zone snowball might be considered adequate, while for other problems such as employment opportunities a four- or five-zone extension might be judged relevant. In any research problem, the failure to attain a complete enumeration of the relevant network can produce significant distortions of the resulting picture of social structure, so it is always advisable to err on the liberal rather than the conservative side in setting boundaries.

The problem of delineating a political communication structure is exemplified in small-world phenomena, captured by the commonly used expression, "It's a small world." When asked to transmit a message to a specified target, even a clerk in Nebraska can reach an unknown stockbroker in Massachusetts with an average of only 5.5 intermediaries (Milgram, 1967; Travers and Milgram, 1969; also Lin et al., 1977, 1978). In short, networks centering on individuals are simultaneously ever expanding and overlapping, so that persons can reach almost anyone

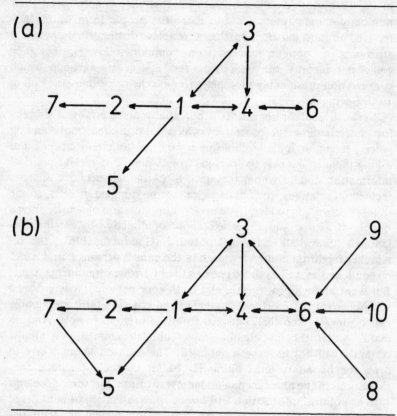

Figure 2 Communication Patterns from Snowball Samples

in large social systems in very few steps (unless the individual is an isolate, i.e., he or she neither gives nor receives political information).

The tendency of real networks to ramify endlessly can pose serious obstacles to reaching substantive conclusions from network data. Assume, for example, that a researcher identifies the structure of political communication on the basis of an initial sample and its first two zones. As shown in Figure 2, actor 1 is one of the initial respondents that has been asked to name other actors to and from whom he or she directly sends and receives information about politics. In turn, the primary contacts of actor 1 (that is, actors 2 through 5) were asked to name their contacts, thereby adding actors 6 and 7 to the network. If the snowballing is terminated at this point, actor 4 would emerge as an opinion leader, since he or she receives information from three network members. Suppose, as shown in Figure 2b, the snowballing were continued by asking actors 6 and 7 to name their political discussion partners. Now, actor 6 appears to be the leader, since he or she has added three new sources and is thus the recipient of four contacts. Subsequent snowballing involving these additional actors could further alter the network structure. The consequences of truncating empirical networks generally will not be as dramatic as this contrived example, but network researchers must be sensitive to the possibility.

Researchers using a nominalist approach commonly study laboratory groups or formally bounded natural groups, such as classrooms or organizational units, as a means of setting limits on networks (see Hallinan, 1978; Homans, 1950; Miller et al., 1981). This strategy, though useful for many purposes, suffers from two potential shortcomings. First, investigation is restricted to relatively small groups, which precludes the kind of large-scale research that characterizes contemporary social science. Second, small-scale settings may solve the boundary problem in appearance only. An analyst who examines the effect of school childrens' classroom interactions on their academic performance, for example, arbitrarily omits relationships that occur outside the classroom (e.g., playground activities). If these latter interactions somehow condition academic performance, conclusions based on in-classroom observations alone may be incorrect. Ultimately, the researcher's theoretical concern must dictate which relationship he or she observes.

A realist approach to specifying the boundaries would apply the criterion of *mutual relevance* (Laumann et al., 1982). This criterion says that only actors who are relevant to each other (as defined by the substantive question) should be included in the social network. Actors whose actions or potential actions are inconsequential, either because they have no interest in the substantive area or because their significance is trivial, are excluded. Application of the consequentiality criterion can be problematic in situations in which actor triviality is difficult to determine beforehand. However, for some populations of actors a priori evidence is available, for example, published statistics on the major firms in an industry or experts' opinions about the leading contenders for a political office.

Knoke and Laumann (1982) used the mutual relevance criterion to delimit the actors in two national policy domains: energy and health. They ignored actors with trivial capacity to affect the behavior of elites within the domain, but recognized that inaction itself is insufficient reason to exclude an actor, since other members of the domain may anticipate the reactions of those not directly involved. To apply the theoretical criterion of mutual relevance, they drew on four types of empirical evidence: (1) *positional* (i.e., formal organizations that have prima facie functions or interests in the domain), (2) *decisional* (organizations or groups appearing at congressional hearings or whose actions and statements are reported in the national press), (3) *reputational* (groups and organizations judged to be influential by a panel of experts), and (4) *relational* (groups and organizations named during the interviews with representatives of organizations obtained by the first three criteria). Though the mutual relevance criterion does not always set precise and definite boundaries, it should be increasingly valuable for the study of large-scale systems, especially those consisting of policymakers.

We have discussed boundary specification first, and for good reason. Much social science research is based on random samples and thus does not require a precise statement about who or what is the focus of investigation. The collection of network data is not "business as usual." Not to specify carefully the boundaries of a social network *before* data collection can lead to dire and costly consequences.

Sampling of Networks in Large Populations

Often it is necessary to make statements about members of a large population, such as a nation's voters or a large community's citizens. In such instances, of course, a complete enumeration of the network is impossible and sampling necessary. Incomplete enumeration always runs the risk of inaccurate measurement of network structure. Unfortunately, the sampling of network data is problematic. Burt stated the problem well (1981: 314-315):

> The network data ignored in a random survey of k% of a population is roughly (1 − k)% so that a random survey of 10% of a population ignores 90% of its network data, a random sample of 25% ignores 75%, and so on. Those lost data are significant. To what extent do the nonsampled persons reciprocate relations directed to them from the sampled respondents? Are respondents the object of strong relations from the system as a whole or are they relatively isolated from the system? How are the nonsampled

persons interconnected, apart from the respondents? Answers to these questions define the network context of the random sample, but the typical survey research design obliterates that context from our view.

Since the number of potential (symmetric) ties in a population of size N is $N(N-1)/2$, even estimating the acquaintance volume (number of people known) in a small town of 10,000 poses insurmountable difficulties, given 50 million potential acquaintance pairs to be investigated.

In short, the problem is this: Network concepts and methods of analysis usually require data on the relations among all actors in the system. When the system is too large to study in its entirety, the only alternative is to estimate those relations of interest as accurately as possible by means of an appropriate network sampling strategy. No completely satisfactory strategy currently exists.

On the positive side, scholars interested in network sampling have made great strides in recent years. Ove Frank (1971, 1978, 1979), a Swedish mathematician, deserves credit for much of the progress in network sampling theory (see also Capobianco, 1970; Proctor, 1979). His work convincingly demonstrated the possibility of estimating the number of ties in a population of size N given a sample size of n.

Because our purpose is to provide an overview of topics for potential collectors of network data, we cannot review Frank's abstruse work. It has influenced others' efforts to bring the collection of network data within the realm of standard data collection procedures. Granovetter (1976) proposed that a researcher draw a random sample of actors, make a list of the respondents' names, and ask each respondent whom he or she knows on the list. The interviewer may simply ask the respondent to indicate acquaintance with the persons on the list or may seek more detailed information such as the nature of the relation, its intensity, duration, and so forth. The observed density of ties between respondents is an unbiased estimate of the density of the entire network from which the sample was drawn. Erickson et al. (1981) demonstrated the feasibility of such sampling and measurement procedures in a moderately large population (a 400-member bridge club).

A potential user of this sampling procedure should be aware of its limitations (Morgan and Rytina, 1977; Granovetter, 1977). It does *not* produce data that can be used at the level of the individual. The procedure's value lies principally in obtaining an estimate of the density of relations in the entire population of actors, using a random sample drawn from a list of names (for example, from a voluntary association's membership roster or from a commerically published directory of a city as large as 100,000 or more residents). It may also prove useful in estimating density within and between subgroups (blacks and whites, for example), although larger samples will probably be necessary to get stable parameters. Moreover, because the procedure consists of asking the respondent about every other person in the sample, the investigator must have access to actual names. Simply identifying households, which is all that standard random surveys require, is inadequate for collecting the necessary network information. Other problems, such as possible interviewee fatigue and missing data, apply more generally to network analysis, and thus we postpone a discussion of them until the following sections.

A second suggested sampling procedure builds on standard random surveys (Beniger, 1976; Burt, 1981). Traditional survey research assumes that selected personal attributes (race, education, age) adequately capture social stratification; i.e., they are good surrogates for actual relations. The essence of the sampling procedure is to collect information from each respondent on the attributes of persons to whom he or she goes for each type of relation studied. The researcher then tries to identify combinations of attributes (including those of the respondents) so that individuals falling into each category have similar relations with others.

Assume, for example, that the researcher begins with two theoretically important attributes: race (white and black) and age (young and old). The two attributes give four possible combinations:

	White (w)	Black (b)
Young (y)		
Old (o)		

Let z_j be the total number of persons that respondent j cites during his or her interview, and let $f_{j,wy}$ be the number of citations to persons who are white and young (to take the first combination). Then the proportion of respondent j's relations that involve persons who are white and young is given as

$$z_{j,wy} = f_{j,wy} / r_j$$

Assume, furthermore, that respondent j is black and old. It is possible to sum relations to white and young people across all respondents who are black and old:

$$f_{(bo,wy)} = \sum_{j=1} (z_{j,wy}) (\delta_{j,bo})$$

where $\delta_{j,bo}$ is a dummy variable equal to zero unless respondent j is black and old. If no black and old respondent cites someone who is white and young, $f_{(bo,wy)}$ equals zero. Dividing by n_{bo}, the number of black and old respondents, gives

$$z_{(do,wy)} = f_{(bo,wy)} / n_{bo}$$

the mean percentage of black and old respondents' citations that are directed toward people who are white and young.

Both respondent j's relations to persons with each of the four attribute combinations and the relations to persons with respondent j's attributes from all other respondents are of interest. The total vector of relations for respondent j, in other words, is

$$z_j = (z_{j,wy},\ z_{j,by},\ z_{j,wo},\ z_{j,bo},\ z_{wy,j},\ z_{by,j},\ z_{wo,j},\ z_{bo,j})$$

where the relations *from* him or her are given by the first four elements, and relations *to* him or her by the last four. Note that $z_{j,wy} \ldots z_{j,bo}$ are based on ties involving respondent j personally, while $z_{wy,j} \ldots z_{bo,j}$ are aggregate relations to his or her combination of attributes rather than to him or her personally. Individuals with identical attributes are *assumed* to be the recipients of identical relations.

What is important to this procedure, then, is not the individual per se, but his or her combination of attributes. The task is to identify combinations such that people with each combination share equivalent relations with others, the others also being defined in terms of attribute combinations. Chapter 4 defines, in precise terms, structurally equivalent relationships.

The most crucial step in this sampling procedure is identification of *all* relevant attributes that presumably stratify the population (our example is simplified, needless to say). To the extent that relevant attributes are omitted, people will be defined as equivalent when in fact they are not. As Burt (1981: 331) puts it, "[A] good deal of iterative data analysis will be required in order to specify the parameter set."

Investigators commonly collect network data without serious atten-tion to sampling and then simply make whatever limited inferences they can from the data. While past reliance on this willy-nilly approach is understandable, given the state of the art, it will undoubtedly become less acceptable as developments in network sampling theory and applications continue.

Finally, a brief observation about the use of statistical inference in network analysis. Conventional statistical analyses of social data are premised on the random sampling of units of observation, for example, in cross-sectional surveys of a population of persons. Network data, consisting of relations among interdependent actors, clearly violate the random sampling assumption and make problematic the application of conventional statistical procedures. At present, the bases for statis-tical inferences from network data are poorly understood, and we can only advise cautious use and hope that the problems will eventually be resolved.

Generic Types of Measures and Reliability

As mentioned in Chapter 2, relations can vary in form and content. Distinctions among relational forms at a general level can be measured as the strength of the link between pairs of actors and their level of joint involvement in the same activities. Strength might be measured as a simple dichotomy (present versus absent connection) or on a finely graded quantitative scale (e.g., the number of interactions over a speci-fied time). Mutual involvement may also be measured with varying degrees of specificity (e.g., the frequency with which contacts are initiated by one actor toward another, such as visiting, helping, in-structing).

Assuming that a researcher has determined the forms of relations and their contents, any of several data collection procedures might be employed. One method, of which the advantages and disadvantages are well known, is direct observation. On the positive side, the data will almost certainly be valid, unless the investigator's participation changes the behavior of the individuals being studied. Similarly, the researcher will understand precisely what the data can mean: Misinterpretation and misrepresentation are unlikely. On the negative side, direct obser-vation is feasible only when the system is small; those who use the laboratory or study relatively contained units (such as a bureau in an organization or a primitive village) will find the method more valuable than those who study large communities or nation-states. Moreover, the behavior about which the researcher collects data may occur infrequently. Thus one anthropologist, in an effort to explain why a birth control method diffused more slowly in an Indian village than did a variety of wheat, had to live in the village for more than a year (Marshall, 1971).

Archival records represent the opposite extreme from direct observation. The researcher is completely removed from the behavior or event being studied, and the data are usually recorded for purposes other than scientific research. Unobtrusive measures obtained from archival records have two unique advantages. First, they can provide network data that would otherwise not be obtainable because people have died, potential respondents refuse interviews, or organizations dissolve themselves. Second, archival data may, under the best of circumstances, span an extended period. Burt (1975; Burt and Lin, 1977), for example, was able to examine individual/corporation relationships from 1877 to 1972 by content analyzing the New York *Times*. Sociologists often use archival data to identify interlocking directorates (i.e., common membership on boards of directors); the underlying assumption is that individuals who sit on the same boards share common interests (Allen, 1974; Burt, 1979; Levine, 1972; Mariolis, 1975).

Given the general popularity of survey data among social scientists, it is hardly surprising that self-reports in surveys are the most common source of information on social networks. Self-reports also pose some of the most severe measurement problems. One potential difficulty is recall. Consider the matter of asking people to identify those with whom they "discuss politics." Because politics is not very central to people's lives, it would be unrealistic to expect perfect recall of political conversations. The problem is not confined to relatively nonsalient topics such as politics. In a series of articles, Bernard and Killworth (1977, 1978; Killworth and Bernard, 1976, 1979) argue that the relations in which people *say* they are involved scarcely resemble those in which they are *actually* involved. Contrasting individuals' reports of interactions with direct observations of behavior, the authors conclude (Bernard et al., 1980: 28):

We are now convinced that cognitive data about communication cannot be used as a proxy for the equivalent behavioral data. This one fundamental conclusion has occurred systematically with a variety of treatments, all as kind to the data as possible. We must therefore recommend unreservedly that any conclusion drawn from the data gathered by the question "who do you talk to" are of no use in understanding the social structure of communication.

This strong indictment, if taken literally, questions the validity of survey-based network data. There are, however, good reasons to believe that Bernard and Killworth's conclusion is not totally warranted. The groups they study are hardly typical: (1) 60 blind persons in the Washington, D.C., area who were linked by teletype; (2) 40 employees of a small social science research office; (3) 34 persons in a graduate program at West Virginia University; (4) 58 residents in a West Virginia fraternity; and (5) 44 amateur radio operators who belonged to the Monongalia Wireless Association. The level of interaction among *all* members of such groups is likely to be uncommonly high; asking individuals to separate very frequent from frequent interactions may be splitting hairs. Moreover, in several instances the form of direct observation consisted of a project researcher walking among the subjects every 15 minutes and coding the frequency with which people contacted each other. This technique, which is used to challenge the validity of survey network data, is itself open to question. To what extent, for example, did the "unobtrusive" observer disrupt ongoing activities? How accurately was he able to record interactions? And what about interactions during the unobserved times (Rogers and Kincaid, 1981: 120-122)? Finally, Burt and Bittner (1981) challenged the analysis that Bernard and Killworth performed on some of their data. The telling tale nonetheless remains: Inaccuracy in the naming of relevant contacts represents a potentially serious source of measurement error.

There are ways to reduce this type of measurement error. The most effective is to be as precise and specific as possible when defining the content of the network being elicited (McCallister and Fischer, 1978). Consider the matter of asking respondents to name those persons with whom they "discuss politics." Political discussion means different things to different people. Some may define it only in terms of candidates and elections, others just in terms of corruption, and still others may include all facets of government (but which level?). The key to measuring equivalent ties is to ask explicitly about candidates and election, *and* corruption, *and* well-defined governmental problems.

Because recall is difficult, especially in an interview situation, the interviewer should provide cues to help the respondent. When asking about people with whom the respondent talks about candidates, for example, the interviewer might ask specifically about people at work, at church, or with whom the respondent spends leisure time.

A final consideration in the collection of survey network data is interviewee fatigue, which might become a problem if a respondent has an extensive network for the particular relation (or multiple relations) under investigation. Faced with naming and providing information on scores of people, the respondent may tire quickly, although practical experience suggests that many respondents will patiently comply for hours on end with researchers' repetitive questioning. Indeed, interviewer fatigue may set in before some respondents call it quits! One frequently used remedy is to ask the respondent to provide two or three names (see Laumann, 1973). This "solution" no longer has credibility among network analysts for the obvious reason that it can severely truncate the networks of actors who are extensively involved with others.

Fischer (1982; McCallister and Fischer, 1978) has refined a technique, developed by Laumann (1966, 1973), that provides detailed network information on up to thirty individuals within 20 minutes of interview time. The first step is to ask the respondent how often (usually, sometimes, or hardly ever) he or she talks about personal matters with someone, and to give the first names of these individuals. The purpose of the second step is to identify network members from a variety of social contexts (work, neighborhood, recreation, and so on). Among the ten name-eliciting questions Fischer uses are: Who would care for the respondents' homes if they went out of town? If they work, with whom do they talk about work decisions? With whom do they talk about hobbies? Throughout the first two steps, the interviewer records the names (no more than ten per question). As part of the third step, the interviewer hands the list to the respondent and asks him or her if there is anyone else important to him or her who is not on the list. With completed list in hand, the interviewer then elicits additional information on each named person, such as sex, the role relation to the respondent, and whether the person lives within a 5-mile radius of the respondent. In the final step, the interviewer selects a subsample of the elicited names (between three and five) and has the respondent fill out a self-administered questionnaire that asks more detailed information (employment and marital status, for example). For each pair of names, the interviewer also asks whether the two "know each other well," which provides a rough measure of the respondent's network density.

Fischer's general format (though perhaps not his specific questions) will be especially valuable to those who intend to begin with a random sample of individuals and obtain detailed information on their networks, as seen by the respondents themselves. It complements, for example, the sampling procedure that Burt proposes. On the other hand, the format will be less useful to investigators who intend to snowball the sample outward since it does not elicit last names or addresses.

Fatigue represents an even greater potential problem when the interviewer gives the respondent a long list of names and asks him or her to indicate which people on the list he or she knows. Yet as we noted earlier, this long and boring task may be necessary if network sampling theory is to be put into practice. Based on their study of competitive bridge players in Toronto, Erickson et al. (1981: 135) concluded that "one can safely use network sampling with lists of at least 130 names. In an interview setting, lists of 150 should be feasible, but lists as long as 200 may well be too great a burden even for willing respondents." However, Knoke and Laumann (1982) found that national energy policy domain elite informants willingly responded to several repeated uses of lists involving more than 250 organization names, preclassified into substantive types (e.g., oil industry, electric utilities, congressional subcommittees). Erickson et al. (1981) also made several recommendations to increase respondent enjoyment and response rates:

(1) Make a brief introductory statement about the purpose of the task in the respondents' own terms (i.e., "we are interested in knowing how people in a community get to know each other").
(2) Include the respondent's name in the name list.
(3) Pretest the relational questions to ensure that they are unambiguous (i.e., "does the person live in Jonestown" rather than "does the person live around here").

Given a list of 130 names, the investigator should allot at least 15 minutes of interview time to complete it.

Missing Data

Investigators should be sensitive to the problem of missing data. As in any research method, respondents may refuse to be interviewed or may not know the answers to certain queries. In conventional cross-sectional surveys, population parameters can frequently be estimated with great accuracy despite a large number of missing cases, assuming that the reasons for the nonresponse are unrelated to the variables under study. For network analysis, however, the consequences of each missing case are more severe, because eliminating a case also removes the N − 1 possible relationships involving other network actors. Obviously, such estimates as network density can be distorted if even a handful of cases is missing. For example, in the national energy policy domain two federal organizations—the Economic Regulatory Administration and the Federal Energy Regulatory Commission—turned out to be major brokers in the flow of policy information. Failure to include these two units among the 200 interviewed in the project could have resulted in a much more fragmented picture of the network than actually emerged.

No failsafe solution to the missing data problem exists. Often one can ask respondents not only about their behavior but about other actors' behavior toward them, for example, not only to whom they give assistance but also from which actors they receive it. Then at least a portion of the missing cases' relations can be reconstructed from others' reports. The potential damage of missing data argues for great care and extraordinary effort in convincing respondents of the importance of participating in the research. Elite and organizational network studies, for instance, have often exceeded 90% response rates, substantially higher than typical household surveys, by using personal letters, telephone contacts, reassurances of confidential treatment, and the respondent's own network contacts as go-betweens (Laumann et al., 1977; Knoke and Wood, 1981).

4. METHODS AND MODELS

Only connect!

—E. M. Forster
Howard's End

This part is concerned with technical matters. We present a variety of procedures for describing and analyzing network data. Two excellent similar reviews are Burt (1980, 1982: ch. 2). The former is organized around a sixfold typology formed by crossing two analytic approaches (relational versus positional) with three levels of actor aggregation into units of analysis (single actors, subgroups, and structured systems). Although this typology is insightful, our present approach is less complex. We begin with an exposition of the elementary terms for visual and algebraic representations of network data and progress through increasingly more sophisticated and complex methods for describing relational systems and testing hypotheses about network structure. We conclude with a look at unresolved issues. Throughout this chapter, the various methods and models are illustrated with a basic set of data, described in the following section.

An Interorganizational Relations Example

The technical procedures will become more meaningful to many readers by applying methods to an illustrative data set. For this purpose, we chose a portion of the network information collected from 95 Indianapolis formal organizations as part of a larger study of voluntary association behavior (Knoke and Wood, 1981; Knoke, 1981, forthcoming). In 1978, questionnaires were sent to leaders of a set of private firms, government agencies, and voluntary associations. The respondents were asked to check off on lists of organizations the ones with which their organizations had engaged in thirteen different types of relationships during the past two years.

For the present monograph, we selected the subset of ten organizations shown in Table 1, and combined four of the types of relations into two networks: (1) to and from which organizations did the respondent's organization send or receive "information about community affairs"; and (2) to and from which organizations did the respondent's organization give or receive "money or other material resources." If either organization in a pair reported that a type of transaction occurred, it was treated as an established exchange relationship. The relations in these two networks are simply "present" or "absent": Neither the level nor the frequency of a transaction is given. Hence the money and the information networks are both *binary* in form. Although as discussed in Chapter 3 network relations can be operationalized in many ways, binary measures provide the most basic form, and many of the analyses described in this chapter can be most usefully applied to this type of relational data.

TABLE 1
Indianapolis Organizations Used in Network Examples

Organization Name	Symbol	Sector*	Influence Reputation
City/County Council	COUN	GOV	5.80
Chamber of Commerce	COMM	VOL	5.80
Board of Education	EDUC	GOV	4.75
Local Industries	INDU	PVT	5.38
Mayor's Office	MAYO	GOV	5.86
Women's Rights Organization	WRO	VOL	2.50
Star-News	NEWS	PVT	6.40
United Way	UWAY	VOL	5.94
Welfare Department	WELF	GOV	4.60
Westend Organization	WEST	VOL	3.50

*GOV = government; VOL = voluntary; PVT = private profit making.

The example is chosen mainly to clarify the use of various analytical techniques and to illustrate how the results can be interpreted in a real situation. The data do not constitute a meaningful, closed system of network actors and no substantive conclusions should be drawn. Rather, the analyses reported below are to be regarded as purely illustrative, based on a deliberately simplified set of actors selected for the sake of clarity.

Table 1 also reports each organization's influence reputation score. A panel of 24 community informants was asked to evaluate all organizations in the project on a 7-point scale according to "how much influence and organization has in *achieving its own objectives*, and not how widespread its influence is in the entire community." Thus informants were asked to judge both the intentions and the actual success of the 95 organizations. For the ten organizations in the present example, the median ratings by the judges are reported, ranging from 6.40 for the newspaper to 2.50 for the Women's Rights Organization (a pseudonym).

Visual Displays

Many terms in network analysis suggest spatial or geometric representations, for example, centrality, periphery, boundary, distance, isolation. Moreno's (1934) pioneering sociometric techniques emphasized construction of the *sociogram*, a two-dimensional diagram displaying the relations observed among actors in a system (e.g., pupils in an elementary school classroom). Although, as noted below, network diagrams have limited usefulness, a didactic advantage can be gained by discussing some basic network terms in diagrammatic format before proceeding to more powerful matrix representations.

In a sociogram, actors are represented by a set of *points*, often labeled by identifying names, letters, or numbers, and the set of relations linking them are represented by *lines* (also, *arcs* or *edges*) drawn between pairs of points having direct connections. These two primitive elements also define a *graph* (Harary, 1959), thus allowing the application of many terms and theorems from graph theory (see Harary et al., 1965; Harary, 1969; Flament, 1963; Behzad and Chartrand, 1971).

Well-constructed visual displays of network relations often have a dramatic impact on viewers and can convey an intuitive feel for the structure of a system. Unfortunately, a virtually limitless number of diagrams can be drawn that contain the same relational information but impart starkly different impressions. Further complicating the situation, as the number of actors and the number of connections increase, parsimony and interpretability of diagrams rapidly dwindle. Sociogram construction is essentially an art form, despite sporadic and unsuccessful efforts to specify invariant procedures. (However, see Klovdahl, 1981, for a proposal to adapt a crystallographic data-plotting program to produce three-dimensional, computer-drawn representations of networks capable of rotation.) For these reasons, our illustration focuses only on the ten-organization diagram of the money exchange network shown in Figure 3. Although only about a quarter of the 90 possible linkages are present in this network, crossing three lines was unavoidable. An attempt to diagram the information exchange network, which had twice as many connections among the ten actors, proved to be futile. A superficial inspection of Figure 3 suggests that the city council, local industries, and the mayor are the main sources of funds, while the United Way, board of education, and welfare department are the main recipients. Additional details of the network structure will be revealed in the following discussion of technical terms.

If all $N^2 - N$ possible lines between the set of N points are present, a graph is *complete*. Obviously, the graph of the money exchange network is far from complete. Two points are *adjacent* if a line directly

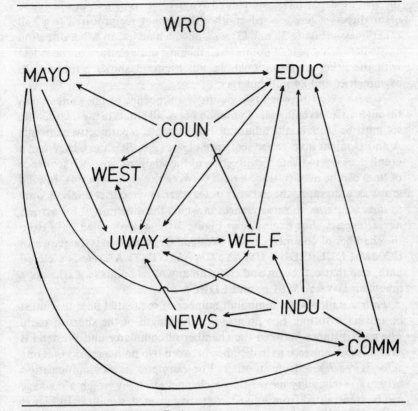

Figure 3 Sociogram of Money Exchange

connects them, although restriction of the diagram to two dimensions frequently requires adjacent points to be located quite far apart (e.g., the mayor and chamber of commerce). In the example, every point is adjacent to at least one other point, except for the Women's Rights Organization (WRO), which is *unconnected*.

The money exchange network is a special type of graph, a *digraph* (directed graph), consisting of the N points linked by a set of *directed lines*. The direction is indicated by the arrowheads; that is, an arrow emerges from the actor initiating the relation and terminates at the actor receiving the relation. In a digraph, three types of lines occur between the $(N^2 - N)/2$ pairs of points: (1) *mutual*, with both points directing lines toward each other, shown by two-headed arrows (e.g., the welfare department and United Way); (2) *asymmetric*, in which one actor directs a line toward another that is not reciprocated (e.g., all other lines in Figure 3); and (3) *null*, in which no line in either direction exists between a pair of points (e.g., the nine null relations of the WRO with the other organizations). In all, Figure 3 shows 1 mutual, 20 asymmetric, and 24 null linkages.

A *path* exists between two points if a sequence of lines links them through an intervening set of points. That is, all points in the intervening set must be sequentially adjacent. For example, a path between points A and D might involve the sequence of lines AB, BC, and CD. When a graph does not indicate the direction of the relations, any such sequence of lines can be used to trace a path between the pairs of points. But if a graph is a digraph, the network researcher may restrict analysis only to *directed paths*, those sequences in which the direction of the arrows never reverses. For example, in Figure 3 the only directed path from the chamber of commerce to the Westend Organization is the sequence COMM-EDUC, EDUC-UWAY, UWAY-WEST. A *cycle* is a closed path, one that can begin and end with any of its points (e.g., the cycle involving UWAY, WELF, and EDUC).

Path distance is the minimum number of sequential lines that must be traversed to link two points, i.e., the length of the shortest path. The path distance between the chamber of commerce and Westend is thus three. A nonzero path distance between two points means that one actor is *reachable* from another. For example, in a communication network reachability means that a channel exists by which a message can be transmitted from a given origin to a given destination. In Figure 3, the *reachable set* for money contributed by local industries includes six other actors (NEWS, COMM, EDUC, WELF, UWAY, WEST), while the reachable set for the mayor includes these same organizations except for the newspaper.

Connectedness is a characteristic of pairs of points, indicating how two points may be linked by directed lines: 0-connected points have no directed lines joining them in either direction (i.e., a pair of 0-connected points is not reachable), 1-connected points are joined by lines disregarding their direction; 2-connected points are joined by a path in one direction but not in another; and 3-connected points are joined by paths in both directions. In Figure 3, the chamber of commerce is 1-connected to the welfare department by a path distance of two (with EDUC or INDU as an intervening point), and is 2-connected by a path of distance 3 (EDUC and UWAY as intervening actors), but no

3-connection occurs between these two actors. Connectedness at the level of the entire graph can be characterized in similar terms: a graph is *stongly connected* if every pair of points in it is 3-connected; it is *unilaterally connected* if every pair is 2-connected; it is *weakly connected* if all pairs are 1-connected; and it is a *disconnected* graph if at least one point is 0-connected (unconnected) with all others. Figure 3 is obviously a disconnected graph, but if WRO is ignored, it is only weakly connected.

Two additional concepts from graph theory applications to networks concern the effects of single changes of elements. Removal of a point involves deleting a point and its associated lines. If a point's removal results in a disconnected graph, the point represents a *cut point* in the network, and the actor presumably plays a liaison or brokerage role in the system. Removal of a line involves deletion of a single connection between two points. If a disconnected graph results, the line represents a *bridge* between system actors. The money-exchange network in Figure 3 contains no instances of cut points or bridges, but the hypothetical networks diagrammed in Figure 4 illustrate these situations.

In network a, actor 4 is a cut point, because his or her removal results in disaggregation of the network into two disconnected subgraphs. In network b, the link between actors 3 and 4 is a bridge, since its removal again would result in two disconnected groups. Granovetter (1973) discussed the importance of "weak ties" as bridges over which information, influence, and resources can be transmitted in complex networks.

Graph theory contains many other concepts and propositions that we cannot begin to consider in this general survey of network methods. A large literature in social psychology uses *signed graphs*, in which the lines have plus or minus signs attached to them to represent positive or negative affect between actors. Theorems about structural balance in such graphs involve multiplying the signed lines in cycles (see Heider, 1946; Cartwright and Harary, 1956; Flament, 1963). Another large literature uses numerical values on the lines to indicate the strength or type of relation between points, for example physical distances or costs of transporting goods between geographical sites (Duffin et al., 1967). These applications are less practical for many noneconomic social science situations in which measures of relations are less sophisticated. In any event, exposition of these advanced techniques is beyond the scope of the present volume, although we shall encounter graph theory ideas below in discussing clique-detection

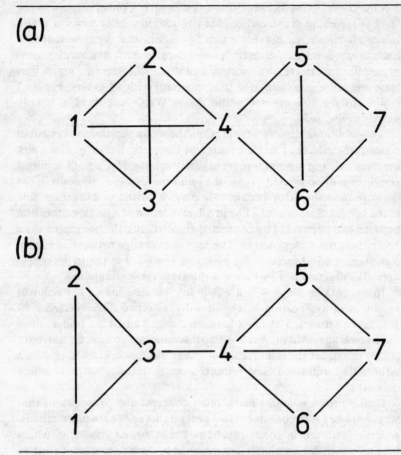

Figure 4   Hypothetical Networks Illustrating (a) Cut Point and (b) Bridge

procedures. Before then, we must consider how visual networks can be represented algebraically.

Matrix Representation

An algebraic representation of network relations can express all the information embedded in a sociogram and can do a great deal more with the data than is possible with a visual format (Forsyth and Katz,

1946; Festinger, 1949). The standard algebraic treatment of network data is a tabular display called a *matrix*, a rectangular array of elements arranged in rows and columns. A matrix is usually denoted by a capital letter marked, e.g., **A**. In typical network applications of matrices, the rows represent system actors and the columns represent the same set of actors in the identical sequence. Thus, matrix **Q**, displaying a specified type of relation among a set of actors, will usually be a square matrix of order (N,N). Sometimes nonsquare matrices will be employed in network analysis, with the M columns standing for other entities (e.g., attributes, events, locations) than the N actors in the rows. Although we cannot devote space in this monograph to such formats, the interested reader is advised to consult Atkin (1974, 1977) and other works (Breiger, 1974; Doreian, 1980, 1981; Gould and Gatrell, 1980).

By convention, in networks of directed relations, the actors arrayed in the matrix rows are initiators of the specified relation and the actors arrayed across the columns are the recipients of the relation. The subscripts i and j, which take integer values from 1 to N (the sample size), are used to reference the elements appearing in the ith row and j^{th} column of a matrix. Because directed relations are seldom perfectly reciprocated in empirical social data, most matrices of directed relations will be *asymmetric*. That is, the element in row i, column j need not be identical to the element in the jth row, i^{th} column. However, if the type of relation is an undirected one, the "from/to" convention is meaningless. In such cases, every tie from i to j is also a tie from j to i and the matrix form will be *symmetric*. As noted in Chapter 3, network researchers often symmetrize their empirical data when it is initially asymmetric if the type of tie they are investigating is conceptually reciprocal or mutual (e.g., a communication channel or a co-worker relation).

The matrix elements are N^2 numerical values that indicate the nature of the linkages between every pair of actors in the network. The simplest elements are *binary* values, with a "1" standing for the occurrence of a tie from actor i to actor j, and a "0" standing for the absence of such a tie between the pair. Binary matrices are also called *adjacency matrices*, because they reveal whether or not any two points in a corresponding sociogram are adjacent. More complex matrix elements might be integer values, for example, to reflect the frequency of contacts between actors, or signed interval or ratio values, for example, to indicate strengths or magnitudes of the specified relation. In general, the variable z_{ijk} represents the value of a relation from the ith actor directed to the jth actor in the kth network. For square matrices, the

Money Exchange **M**

	C O U N	C O M M	E D U C	I N D U	M A Y O	W R O	N E W S	U W A Y	W E L F	W E S T
COUN	0	0	1	0	1	0	0	1	1	1
COMM	0	0	1	0	0	0	0	0	0	0
EDUC	0	0	0	0	0	0	0	1	0	0
INDU	0	1	1	0	0	0	1	1	1	0
MAYO	0	1	1	0	0	0	0	1	1	0
WRO	0	0	0	0	0	0	0	0	0	0
NEWS	0	1	0	0	0	0	0	1	0	0
UWAY	0	0	0	0	0	0	0	0	1	1
WELF	0	0	1	0	0	0	0	1	0	0
WEST	0	0	0	0	0	0	0	0	0	0

Information Exchange **I**

	C O U N	C O M M	E D U C	I N D U	M A Y O	W R O	N E W S	U W A Y	W E L F	W E S T
COUN	0	1	0	0	1	0	1	0	1	0
COMM	1	0	1	1	1	0	1	1	1	0
EDUC	0	1	0	1	1	1	1	0	0	1
INDU	1	1	0	0	1	0	1	0	0	0
MAYO	1	1	1	1	0	0	1	1	1	1
WRO	0	0	1	0	0	0	1	0	1	0
NEWS	0	1	0	1	1	0	0	0	0	0
UWAY	1	1	0	1	1	0	1	0	1	0
WELF	0	1	0	0	1	0	1	0	0	0
WEST	1	1	1	0	1	0	1	0	0	0

Figure 5   Interorganizational Networks in Matrix Format

diagonal values (the N, z_{iik} elements) correspond to self-directed relations. As network operationalizations often do not allow for meaningful self-choices, $z_{iik} = 0$ in many matrix representations.

Figure 5 shows the binary matrix representations for both example networks, the money exchange (**M**) and information exchange (**I**) systems among the ten organizations. Note that the labels for the rows and columns are *not* part of the matrix, but are included for the reader's convenience. Matrix **M** is essentially an algebraic translation of Figure 3. For example, reading across the first row, one can see that the city/county council gave money to five organizations, while reading down the first column, the council received money from none. Similarly, the WRO's isolation from all nine other groups is evident in its row and column of solid 0s. Turning to Matrix **I**, we observe immediately that it contains a larger number of directed ties and that every actor sends and receives information with at least one other organization.

Some simple descriptive statistics are obtained by summing across matrix entries. The *degree of a point* is the integer count or number of other actors with which a given actor has direct contact. The *outdegree* of actor i is the number (or proportion) of relations from that actor to all others, that is, the sum of 1s within actor i's row:

$$\text{Outdegree}_{ik} = \sum_{j=1}^{N} z_{ijk} = z_{i \cdot k}$$

Similarly, actor j's *indegree* is the number (or proportion) of relations received by actor j from all others, calculated as the sum of 1s within actor j's column:

$$\text{Indegree}_{jk} = \sum_{i=1}^{N} z_{ijk} = z_{\cdot jk}$$

Particularly in the case in which the relation is an affective tie (e.g., liking, friendship), an actor's indegree measures his or her popularity within the network. In a corresponding sociogram, such network "stars" are evident as the recipients of many directed arrows from the other points.

Density, a characteristic of the entire network, is a proportion that is calculated as the number of all ties occurring in the matrix divided by the number of all possible ties ($N^2 - N$, if self-directed relations are not permissible):

$$\text{Density}_k = \frac{\sum_{i=1}^{N} \sum_{j=1}^{N} z_{ijk}}{N^2 - N} \qquad i \neq j$$

Density ranges between 0 and 1.00, representing the extremes of a totally disconnected or totally connected graph.

In matrix **I**, the outdegrees range from 3 for WRO to 8 for the mayor, and the indegrees range from 1 for WRO to 9 for the newspaper. The density of network **I** is 0.54, considerably higher than the density of **M** at 0.24.

Expressing network relations in matrix form yields substantial benefits over visual display. Perhaps foremost, it facilitates the analysis of indirect relations. The indirect connections among a set of N actors in a network can be uncovered by raising an adjacency matrix **K** to successive powers, that is, by multiplying the matrix of binary ties by itself T times. The resulting elements in K^T give the number of T-step connections leading from actor i to actor j. In matrix multiplication, each element in the resulting (N,N) product matrix is found by a pairwise multiplication and summation of the corresponding row and column vectors in the original matrix. For example, in multiplying matrix **M** by itself, the value of the element in row 1, column 8 of M^2 is found by multiplying the corresponding ten elements in the first row and the eighth column of matrix **M**, then summing these ten products:

$$(0)(1) + (0)(0) + (1)(1) + (0)(1) + (1)(1) + (0)(0) + (0)(1)$$

$$+ (1)(0) + (1)(1) + (1)(0) = 3$$

Thus, there are three two-step connections between COUN and UWAY, through EDUC, MAYO, or WELF, a fact that can easily be verified by inspection of Figure 3, but which can be tedious and time-consuming for a large matrix without resort to matrix multiplication. Figure 6 displays the complete results of raising **M** to the second and to the sixth powers, respectively. In the 6-step matrix, we see that ten distinct paths of length six connect COUN to UWAY, although all are redundant paths, such as the COUN-WELF-EDUC-UWAY-WELF-EDUC-UWAY sequence.

Apart from showing how specific pairs of actors are indirectly tied together, the set of T-step matrices reveals something about the overall structure of the network. For example, Figure 6 shows that the majority of pairs are unreachable in the money network even through lengthy chains. The reason for this pattern seems to be that organizations specialize as sources or sinks of funds, with relatively few transmitters. In contrast, upon raising the information exchange network, **I**, to the

M^2

	C O U N	C O M M	E D U C	I N D U	M A Y O	W R O	N E W S	U W A Y	W E L F	W E S T
COUN	0	1	2	0	0	0	0	3	2	1
COMM	0	0	0	0	0	0	0	1	0	0
EDUC	0	0	0	0	0	0	0	0	1	1
INDU	0	1	2	0	0	0	0	3	1	1
MAYO	0	0	2	0	0	0	0	2	1	1
WRO	0	0	0	0	0	0	0	0	0	0
NEWS	0	0	1	0	0	0	0	0	1	1
UWAY	0	0	1	0	0	0	0	1	0	0
WELF	0	0	0	0	0	0	0	1	1	1
WEST	0	0	0	0	0	0	0	0	0	0

M^6

	C O U N	C O M M	E D U C	I N D U	M A Y O	W R O	N E W S	U W A Y	W E L F	W E S T
COUN	0	0	6	0	0	0	0	10	7	7
COMM	0	0	1	0	0	0	0	1	1	1
EDUC	0	0	1	0	0	0	0	2	1	1
INDU	0	0	5	0	0	0	0	8	6	6
MAYO	0	0	3	0	0	0	0	6	5	5
WRO	0	0	0	0	0	0	0	0	0	0
NEWS	0	0	1	0	0	0	0	3	2	2
UWAY	0	0	1	0	0	0	0	2	2	2
WELF	0	0	2	0	0	0	0	3	2	2
WEST	0	0	0	0	0	0	0	0	0	0

Figure 6   Two- and Six-Step Connections in Money Exchange Network

third power, every organization has one or more paths to every other organization, indicating complete reachability in this network in three or fewer steps.

Two new matrices can be calculated to display the reachabilities and path distances among network actors. The first procedure sums a series of K^T matrices to produce a *reachability matrix*, R^T, whose elements show whether or not actor i can reach actor j in T or fewer steps:

$$R^T = K + K^2 + K^3 + \ldots + K^T$$

(Matrix addition simply involves adding together the numerical values of the corresponding i, j elements of each matrix in the sum.) The elements r_{ijk} of R^T are counts of the total number of connections between pairs of actors involving T or fewer steps. A zero element in R^T means that that pair of actors is not reachable in T or fewer steps, although reachability may occur in chains of greater length.

The second procedure results in a *path distance matrix*, D^T, whose elements d_{ijk} reveal the shortest chains linking actors i and j in the kth network. It is calculated as:

$$D^T = K + K^{2'} + K^{3'} + \ldots + K^{T'}$$

where $K^{T'}$ is K^T in which all nonzero elements are set equal to T except for those elements that have been replaced by zeros because they were nonzero in matrix K raised to some power less than T. The diagonal elements always remain zero in the calculation. The longest path distance in a network will equal T when K^{T+1} has no zero elements in lower powers of the matrix. The D^T procedure excludes redundant connections that occur in R^T and thus may be preferred as a relational operationalization. Figure 7 illustrates path distance matrices for both M and I. Notice that although any reachable pair requires three or fewer steps in each matrix and every actor can reach every other actor in the information exchange network, only about a third of the pairs are reachable in the money exchange network.

At times, a normalization of path distances may be useful, especially when the network analyst is interested in comparing systems with different densities or different numbers of actors. Lincoln and Miller (1979) provided a simple equation for changing the elements of D^T to *proximities*:

$$p_{ijk} = 1 - \frac{d_{ijk} - 1}{d_{max}}$$

M

	COUN	COMM	EDUC	INDU	MAYO	WRO	NEWS	UWAY	WELF	WEST
COUN	0	2	1	0	1	0	0	1	1	1
COMM	0	0	1	0	0	0	0	2	3	3
EDUC	0	0	0	0	0	0	0	1	2	2
INDU	0	1	1	0	0	0	1	1	1	2
MAYO	0	1	1	0	0	0	0	1	1	3
WRO	0	0	0	0	0	0	0	0	0	0
NEWS	0	1	2	0	0	0	0	1	2	2
UWAY	0	0	2	0	0	0	0	0	1	1
WELF	0	0	1	0	0	0	0	1	0	2
WEST	0	0	0	0	0	0	0	0	0	0

I

	COUN	COMM	EDUC	INDU	MAYO	WRO	NEWS	UWAY	WELF	WEST
COUN	0	1	2	2	1	3	1	2	1	2
COMM	1	0	1	1	1	2	1	1	1	2
EDUC	2	1	0	1	1	1	1	2	2	1
INDU	1	1	2	0	1	3	1	2	2	2
MAYO	1	1	1	1	0	2	1	1	1	1
WRO	3	2	1	2	2	0	1	3	1	2
NEWS	2	1	2	1	1	3	0	2	2	2
UWAY	1	1	2	1	1	3	1	0	1	2
WELF	2	1	2	2	1	3	1	2	0	2
WEST	1	1	1	2	1	2	1	2	2	0

Figure 7 Path Distance Matrices for Money and Information Exchange Networks

where d_{max} is the largest path distance observed in the kth network between any reachable pair. When two actors are directly connected (i.e., their path distance is 1), the proximity value is 1. When two actors are unconnected (their path distance value is 0), p_{ijk} is set equal to 0. Other distances then take on values ranging between 0 and 1, with larger proximities occurring when fewer intervening links are required for i to reach j.

Other methods proposed to normalize the connections in a matrix include: (a) requiring each actor's choices to sum to a total of 1 (Hubbell, 1965); (b) subjecting path distances to smallest space analysis to measure essential aspects of relational intensity (Laumann and Pappi, 1976); (c) using path distances in overlapping social circles (Alba and Kadushin, 1976); and (d) basing normalization on a nonlinear function of decreasing relational intensity with increasing path distance (Burt, 1982: 28-29).

The methods described above for calculating reachability, path distance, and proximity in matrix representations of network data focus on the relation of one actor to another as a dyad. They do not consider the other N − 2 actors except insofar as those others are necessary to complete the chain of steps from actor i to actor j. In the sections below we investigate distance measures that take into account the relations among the other actors in the network. The following section lays the groundwork by considering some indicators of actors' positions in networks.

Indices for Actors and Networks

Many different indices can be computed from matrices to summarize characteristics for both individual actors and entire networks. The potential set of indices seems limited only by analysts' imaginations, but space limitations allow coverage of just the more familiar and widely used indices.

An index of *network cohesion*, G, divides the number of mutual choices in a binary matrix of directed ties by the maximum possible number of such choices:

$$G = \frac{\sum\limits_{i=1}^{N} \sum\limits_{j=1}^{N} (z_{ijk} + z_{jik})}{(N^2 - N)/2} \qquad i \neq j$$

where the term $(z_{ijk} + z_{jik})$ takes the value of 1 if both elements are 1s; otherwise it takes the value of 0. The cohesion index ranges from 0 to 1.0, with larger values indicating that a greater proportion of network relations are reciprocated. Note that the network cohesion index resembles the density measure described above, the difference being that asymmetric ties are counted in the latter but ignored in the former.

An index of *network multiplicity*, M, is based on two or more networks of relations for the same set of N actors. A tie between actors i and j is said to be *multiplex* if $z_{ijk} = 1$ in some specified proportion of the $k = 2 \ldots K$ networks under consideration. For example, if actor i cites actor j in a friendship network actor i also cites actor j in the advice-giving network, the money-lending network, the favor-trading network, and so on. In its most general form, network multiplexity may be calculated as:

$$M = \frac{\sum\limits_{i=1}^{N} \sum\limits_{j=1}^{N} z_{ij}(m)}{N^2 - N} \qquad i \neq j$$

where $z_{ij}(m)$ is 0 unless multiple z_{ijk} are nonzero from i to j, in which case $z_{ij}(m)$ equals 1. The network multiplicity index varies from 0 to 1.0, reflecting the proportion of all possible pairs of actors that have the specified level of multiplex ties.

At the individual actor level, *actor multiplexity* can be measured as the proportion of an actor's ties with all other $N - 1$ actors in the system that are multiplex across K networks. Its formula is:

$$M_i' = \frac{\sum\limits_{j=1}^{N} \sum\limits_{k=1}^{K} z_{ijk}(m)}{N - 1}$$

again, where the $z_{ijk}(m)$ value is 1 if actor i has the requisite number of links with a given actor j across the K networks, and is 0 if otherwise.

A related index at the level of the individual actor is an actor's *ego network density*, D_E, which extends to the individual the concept of network density considered in the previous section. Actor i's ego network consists of that subset among the other $N - 1$ system actors with which the actor i has direct connections. This set is also called the "first star" or "primary star" (of course, actors who are disconnected from a network have no ego network and their density can be considered either to be zero or undefined). If there are n_E alters in actor i's ego network for the kth matrix, the density index is calculated as:

$$D_E = \frac{\sum\limits_{i=1}^{n_E} \sum\limits_{j=1}^{n_E} z_{ijk}}{(n_E^2 - n_E)} \qquad i \neq j$$

which gives the proportion of potential linkages among ego's alters that actually occur.

The various indices of network *centrality* trace their origins to Bavelas's (1950) and Leavitt's (1951) research on the effects of social structure in human communication. They introduced the idea that the more central an actor, the greater his or her degree of involvement in all the network relations. The simplest centrality index for actor i is a ratio of the aggregate relations involving i over all relations in a network, i.e., the proportion of all network relations that involve i:

$$C_i = \frac{\sum\limits_{j=1}^{N} (z_{ij} + z_{ji})}{\sum\limits_{i=1}^{N} \sum\limits_{j=1}^{N} z_{ij}} \qquad i \neq j$$

For example, in the money exchange network (**M**) the United Way's centrality score is 0.36 and the mayor's is 0.23, but in the information exchange network (**I**) their centrality scores are 0.16 and 0.33, respectively.

Freeman's (1979) review identified nine distinct centrality indices based on three structural properties possessed by the center of a star network (a star is a configuration in which a point is connected to the $N - 1$ other points, which are themselves unconnected). The interested reader is referred to the article for further details, as we can present only two centrality indices based on "betweenness," which Freeman (1979: 237) asserts provide "'finer grained' measures than the others." Moreover, the centrality indices below are restricted to binary, symmetric data.

The shortest path that links a pair of points, i and j, in a network is called a *geodesic*. Any point or points that fall on a geodesic(s) linking a pair of points is said to stand *between* the two endpoints. For example, in Figure 4a, point 4 lies between 3 and 6. For the endpoints 4 and 7, two geodesics (of path distance two) exist, with points 5 and 6 lying between or on either one. If Figure 4a represents a network of communication channels, then the between points have the potential to control, disrupt, or distort the flow of information between the endpoints, either entirely as in the first instance or with some partial control as in the latter instance, where alternative geodesics could carry the communication.

Assuming that two endpoints i and j are indifferent as to which geodesic is used, the probability of using any one is $1/g_{ij}$ where g_{ij} is the number of geodesics linking i and j. If actor m lies between the endpoints of a geodesic, the number of such geodesics that involve m is g_{imj}. Freeman (1977) showed that the maximum value on an index of partial betweenness of a point is attained only by the central point in a star network. That value is $(N^2 - 3N + 2)/2$. Hence an appropriate index of *relative centrality* for point m is the ratio:

$$C'_B(p_m) = \frac{2 \displaystyle\sum_{i<j}^{N} \sum^{N} \frac{g_{imj}}{g_{ij}}}{N^2 - 3N + 2} \qquad i \neq j$$

Values range between 0 and 1, with higher scores indicating greater actor centrality relative to other network members. Matrix methods for locating and counting the geodesics in large networks are detailed in Harary et al. (1965: 134-141) and require a computer program to process the data. The relative centrality index can be calculated only on binary symmetric matrices, but can be applied to disconnected as well as connected graphs. For other actor centrality indices based on the degree of a point (the number of other points in direct contact with i) and closeness of a point (path distances between points), consult Freeman (1979).

The betweenness concept of centrality can also be applied to an entire network. An index of *centralization* is based on the difference

between the centrality score of the most central actor and that of the
N – 1 other actors:

$$C_B = \frac{\sum\limits_{i=1}^{N} (C_B(p^*) - C_B(p_i))}{N^3 - 4N^2 + 5N - 2}$$

where $C_B(p^*)$ is the relative centrality score of the most central point.
This index takes its greatest value, 1.0, for a network star in which a
single actor dominates the connections among all others, and it takes
its smallest value, 0, in circle or all-channel (complete) graphs in which
no actor is structurally distinct from any other.

The final indices considered in this section measure the *prestige* (p_i)
of actors within the network. An actor has greater prestige to the degree
that other system actors show deference to him or her in their relation.
Practically, this definition means that prestigious actors will more
often tend to receive than to initiate linkages, that is, to be chosen
rather than choosers. As with centrality, several alternative operationalizations of prestige are possible. The simplest, based on direct ties
only, is an actor's indegree (see preceding section) or, alternatively, the
proportion of all ties in the system that are directed toward an actor.
Better indices of prestige take into account indirect linkages as well
as direct ties.

Lin (1976: 340-349) first defines an actor's *influence domain* (I_i) as
the total number of actors that directly or indirectly send relations to
an individual. Next, the individual's centrality (C_i) is defined as the
mean distance to all actors in the influence domain, on the assumption
that each linkage in a chain has the same magnitude. Actor i's prestige
is then calculated as:

$$p_i = \frac{I_i}{(C_i)(N - 1)}$$

If centrality is zero, that is, if an actor is disconnected, the actor's prestige is also zero. This index varies between zero and one, with higher
values indicating greater prestige and the maximum attained when
all other actors directly send relations to actor i.

A more sophisticated prestige index corporates the prestige of the actors sending ties to actor i. Each element in the column vector of actor i in matrix **K** is multiplied by the prestige scores of the N – 1 other actors (subscripted j) and the sum of these products is actor i's prestige score:

$$p_i = \sum_{j=1}^{N-1} p_j z_{jik}$$

Thus, actor i's prestige is higher to the extent that it receives many ties directed to it by many other prestigious actors who are themselves the recipients of directed ties from many other actors. The scores thereby take indirect as well as direct linkages into account. Note that, in a matrix of symmetric relations, the prestige score is also a centrality measure (see Knoke and Burt, 1982). Because prestige scores appear on both sides of the equation, a simultaneous solution to the N equations is required, using a computer algorithm.

In matrix algebra notation, the system of equations is:

$$O = P'(Z - I)$$

where **P'** is a vector of N prestige scores, **Z** is the (N,N) matrix of observed direct relations, and **I** is the identity matrix (a square matrix with 1s on the main diagonal and 0s elsewhere). If the relations in **Z** are normalized so that the matrix is column stochastic (elements are nonnegative and sum to 1.0 within columns), then the equation is the "characteristic equation" of matrix **Z** (van der Geer, 1971: 64). The set of prestige scores for all actors can then be calculated (by computer) as the first eigenvector.

A network analyst's choice among various indices for individual actors or entire networks is not a simple decision, but can be revealed only after careful consideration of the conceptual, substantive, and empirical features of the problem at hand. For instance, the decision to select a measure of actor centrality or prestige hinges in large part on whether the relations measured are truly reciprocal (sent and received) or genuinely asymmetric (received only), and on whether or not the quality of the other actors' network location should be taken into account (see Knoke and Burt, 1982, for a detailed discussion). Because the grounds for index usage constantly change across situations, we can offer no universal rules for choice, but only counsel the network analyst to proceed only after thorough investigation of the implications of using alternative measures.

Clique Detection

The preceding sections considered network aspects of individual actors and of entire systems. In this and subsequent sections, attention shifts to methods for partitioning networks into subgroup components. Two predominant methods for determining the number and composition of subsets are the clique-detection approach, considered in this section, and the structural equivalence approach, presented in the next section.

The *clique* is a central concept in much small group research, and it has been a mainstay of theoretical and empirical investigations for more than three decades. Many definitions have been proffered over the years by different analysts (Harary, 1959; Lindzey and Borgatta, 1954), but most incorporate the idea that a clique is a highly cohesive subset of actors within a network. In some versions, all or most clique members possess a specified relation (e.g., friendship, communication), while in other versions clique-mates are characterized as having more numerous or more intense relations with each other than with non-clique actors. In either case, the implicit proposition motivating clique analysis is that actors who maintain especially cohesive bonds among themselves are more likely to perform similarly (e.g., to share information, to develop similar preferences, to act in concert).

Following Festinger (1949) and Luce and Perry (1949), the most stringent and restrictive formal definition of a clique is a *maximal complete subgraph*, a set of completely linked points not contained within a larger, completely linked set. Cartwright and Harary (1956) added the further stipulation that a clique include at least three members. For an undirected graph, the minimum configuration for a clique is three points connected by three lines. For digraphs, the smallest clique consists of three actors each in mutual relation (i.e., six directed linkages among the three points); in other words, a clique is a strongly connected subset of digraph members. Every pair of actors in a clique is adjacent, while adding any other network actor to the clique will make it less than 3-connected. More generally, if clique size is n, digraph clique will have $(n^2 - n)$ directed relations, and an undirected graph clique will have $(n^2 - n)/2$ lines.

Although the digraph in Figure 3 contains no cliques under this definition, the undirected graph in Figure 4a contains three such cliques: (1) points 1, 2, 3, and 4; (2) points 4, 5, and 6; and (3) points 5, 6, and 7. As this illustration implies, many networks do not partition neatly into unique, nonoverlapping cliques. The latter occurrence suggests either a disjointed nonsystem or factions in overt conflict (Roistacher, 1974: 133).

The basic methodological question is: Given a matrix K of N actors, how can a researcher determine the number of cliques, their constituent actors, and patterns of clique overlap? The stringent maximal complete subgraph definition and pre-computer-era difficulty in processing large networks soon led network researchers to develop more ad hoc methods for clique detection (Harary and Ross, 1957; McQuitty, 1957; MacRae, 1960; Coleman and MacRae, 1960; Hubbell, 1965; Doreian, 1969; Lankford, 1974). These procedures had their own computational difficulties, especially with very large matrices, and their theoretical foundations were often obscure (Alba and Moore, 1978). With the rise of powerful computers, algorithms for locating all maximal complete subgraphs were eventually written (Augustson and Minker, 1970).

By that time, however, the completeness criterion had come to be seen as overly restrictive for many substantive applications. A subset of actors might fail to be identified as a clique because only a few relations among its members were lacking. Realistically, measurement error could result in some truly strong and reciprocated linkages going unmeasured in the data collection phase. Furthermore, as every clique member has a path distance one to every other member, no variation in internal clique structure occurs. Clearly, some relaxation of the maximal complete subgraph criterion seemed desirable, thus allowing a strongly connected clique to be augmented by more peripheral actors that might not have reciprocal ties to all others in the clique.

Proposed alternative criteria for clique detection have mostly been variants of the *maximal strong component* concept from graph theory (Harary et al., 1965: 53-55). A maximal strong component is a network subgroup in which each actor can at least reach every other actor directly or indirectly and no further actors can be added without losing this mutual reachability. Actors i and j can be joined together into a clique if the smaller of z_{ij} and z_{ji} is at least greater than some criterion alpha (or greater than zero for binary matrices). Hubbell (1965) and Doreian (1969) described clique-detection procedures using this relaxed criterion, and Laumann and Pappi (1976: 102-105) applied it in investigating networks among elites in a small German city.

Among the more noteworthy uses of the maximal strong component definition is to locate *n-cliques* (Luce, 1950). Actors form an n-clique if the relations between all pairs are measured as the reciprocal of their path distances and the smaller value for any pair of actors exceeds $1/(n + 1)$. Thus every member of an n-clique can reach every other in n or fewer binary links. An n-clique allows for indirect connections through intermediary actors but limits the maximum distance across which such indirect interactions can occur. Luce's definition permits n-clique members to be connected via intermediaries that are not themselves clique members. Alba (1973) suggested further restricting a clique to be an n-clique in which every pair of actors is connected by a geodesic (a shortest path, see above) composed solely of other clique members.

Another relaxation of the stringent clique definition is the *k-plex clique* (Seidman and Foster, 1978). A k-plex structure is a graph with n points in which each point is connected by a path of length 1 to at least $n - k$ of the other points. Thus every actor of a k-plex has maximum strong relations with all except k clique members. Because complete graphs are 1-plexes, a true clique in the maximal complete subgraph definition is a special case of the k-plex approach. But in permitting more indirectly connected actors into the k-plex clique, the method allows for internal variation in clique structure.

The k-plex definition is consistent with the concept of a *social circle*, a set of actors with shared interests having direct or minimally indirect linkages with each other (Kadushin, 1966, 1968; also Alba and Kadushin, 1976). As operationalized by Alba and Moore (1978), detection of social circles begins with finding all maximal complete subgraph cliques and then successively aggregating them when they overlap to a specified degree. For example, all simple cliques of three or more actors are first identified; then cliques that differ by a single member are joined. Next, if three quarters of the members of a smaller group also belong to a larger circle or clique, the two are merged. (The 75% overlap is arbitrary, and Alba and Moore considered other levels before deciding on this value as most suitable for the network they were analyzing.) Subsequent aggregations, using the same or different criteria of overlapping strong components, can be made until the researcher decides closure is warranted on theoretical or substantive grounds. The resultant social circles thus are composed of actors that, while not having maximum strength relations with each other nor even mutual reachability, are still required to maintain contacts with a large proportion of the other circle members.

Most of the clique-detection procedures mentioned above are sufficiently complex as to require computer implementation for application to empirical research. Thus, space limitations prevent us from providing detailed explanations of the steps involved in moving from matrix data on direct relations to the identification of cliques, n-cliques, k-plexes, and social circles. Readers are urged to consult the original sources cited above.

Many of the clique-detection methods are not concerned with inter-clique relations. Except for the n-clique technique, ties to nonclique actors are generally ignored. This failure to take into account the full set of relations among all network actors is a major criticism leveled against the clique approach to network partitioning by researchers who prefer the structural equivalence approach.

Structural Equivalence

The second basic approach to partitioning network actors into subgroups involves the application of a structural equivalance criterion to their relations. As briefly described in Chapter 2, actors are aggregated into a jointly occupied position to the extent that they have a common set of linkages to other system actors. More formally, two objects a and b of a set C are *structurally equivalent* if, for any given relation R and any object x of C, aRx if and only if bRx, and xRa if and only if xRb. "In other words, a is structurally equivalent to b if a relates to every object x of C in exactly the same way as b does. From the point of view of the logic of the structure, then a and b are absolutely equivalent, they are substitutable" (Lorrain and White, 1971: 63).

The structural equivalence criterion requires a pair of actors to have exactly identical patterns of relations with the N - 2 other actors in the network in order to be placed together in the same network position. For most empirical purposes, this criterion is too stringent and impractical, just as the maximal complete subgraph definition of a clique proved to be too restrictive. As shown below, in practice network researchers typically relax the criterion of strong structural equivalence, grouping actors in the same positions on the basis of their similarity of relations to other actors. A structural equivalence criterion for placing a pair of actors in the same position takes into account not their relations to each other (as in the clique-detection approach), but only their relations with the other system actors. Indeed, structural equivalence procedures for partitioning a set of network actors do not require any members of the equivalent subset to maintain relations with each other. Such empirical results do occur and have meaningful interpretations. Thus the most obvious contrast between the clique-detection and the structural equivalence methods lies in their differential emphasis on relations within or between subgroup actors.

Cliques have usually been identified for single networks, while substantive applications of structural equivalence to multiple networks have implied that the latter technique is preferable for analyses of multiple network systems. However, the structural equivalence applications simply sum comparisons across networks, disregarding substantive grounds for the summation. Comparable procedures in clique-detection would also simply add relations among actors across several networks to obtain an aggregate relation matrix for analysis. Hence both approaches are equally well (or ill) suited to multiple network data.

An appreciation of the structural equivalence approach can be gained by a detailed examination, with examples from the **I** and **M** matrices, of its two most popular operationalizations: as continuous and as discrete distance measures. As the former conceptualization subsumes the latter (Burt, 1977a: 124-127), we begin with the more general method of measuring structural equivalence in continuous distance terms.

CONTINUOUS DISTANCE

The key assumption in this operationalization of structural equivalence is that distance between a pair of actors is measurable in terms of dissimilarity in their patterns of relations with other system actors. If they have exactly identical relations with the others, their distance is zero and, as noted above, they occupy an identical point in the social space. As the pair of actors have increasingly different patterns of ties with the others, they are increasingly more distant from each other in the social space. Conceptualizing a social space in Euclidean terms, the distance between actors i and j (d_{ij} and d_{ji}, where distances are symmetric) equals the square root of the sum of squared differences across all third actors q:

$$d_{ij} = d_{ji} = \sqrt{\sum_{q=1}^{N} (z_{iq} - z_{jq})^2 + (z_{qi} - z_{qj})^2}$$

where $(z_{iq} - z_{jq})$ is the difference between the two actors in the relations they initiate with a thrid actor (i.e., a pair of elements in rows i and j of matrix **K**), and $(z_{qi} - z_{qj})$ is the discrepancy in relations received from a third actor (i.e., a pair of elements found in columns i and j of matrix **K**).

This distance metric readily generalizes to more than one network of relations by summing values across $K \geqslant 2$ matrices involving the same set of N system actors:

$$d_{ij} = d_{ji} = \sqrt{\sum_{k=1}^{K} \sum_{q=1}^{N} (z_{iq} - z_{jq})^2 + (z_{qi} - z_{qj})^2}$$

In either case, regardless of the number of matrices of relations over which social role distance is calculated, the result is an $N \times N$ symmetric matrix of distances between every pair of actors. Main diagonal elements are zero, to reflect no distance of any actor from itself.

To illustrate the use of these formulas, we will calculate the distance between the United Way and the welfare department, using both the information and money exchange networks shown in Figure 5 above. In effect, we first pull out the two pairs of row vectors from both matrices and place them parallel to each other:

	Money	Information
UWAY	0 0 0 0 0 0 0 0 <u>1</u> 1	1 1 0 1 1 0 1 0 <u>1</u> 0
WELF	0 0 1 0 0 0 0 <u>1</u> 0 0	0 1 0 0 1 0 1 0 <u>0</u> 0

The underlined z's are the direct relations between the two actors. Under some specifications of the distance, these relations may be ignored in calculating distance between pairs of actors. If they are included, as they will be here, they should not be double-counted when taking the sum of differences across the pair of columns (below). Next, the pairwise differences in the row vector elements are formed, squared, and summed for both matrices:

$$0+0+1+0+0+0+0+1+1+1 \qquad +1+0+0+1+0+0+0+0+1+0 = 7$$

Turning to the columns for the two actors, we pull out the pair of vectors from both matrices:

UWAY	WELF
1	1
0	0
1	0
1	1
1	1
0	0
1	0
*	*
*	*
0	0
0	1
1	1
0	0
0	0
1	1
0	1
0	0
*	*
*	*
0	0

The asterisks replace the redundant pairs of relations that have already been used in the row differences. Taking the sum of squared differences between column elements yields 4. The square root of the sum of 7 and 4 is 3.317, the social role distance between the United Way and the welfare department for the two matrices.

D

	C O U N	C O M M	E D U C	I N D U	M A Y O	W R O	N E W S	U W A Y	W E L F	W E S T
COUN	0.00	3.87	3.87	3.00	3.46	3.74	3.46	3.46	3.16	3.61
COMM	3.87	0.00	4.24	3.74	3.00	3.87	3.32	3.87	3.87	3.87
EDUC	3.87	4.24	0.00	4.00	4.24	4.00	3.46	3.32	3.00	3.61
INDU	3.00	3.74	4.00	0.00	3.30	3.74	3.16	3.74	3.32	3.32
MAYO	3.46	3.00	4.24	3.32	0.00	4.12	3.46	4.24	4.00	4.00
WRO	3.74	3.87	4.00	3.74	4.12	0.00	4.00	4.00	3.87	2.65
NEWS	3.46	3.32	3.46	3.16	3.46	4.00	0.00	4.12	3.16	3.87
UWAY	3.46	3.87	3.32	3.74	4.24	4.00	4.12	0.00	3.32	3.46
WELF	3.16	3.87	3.00	3.32	4.00	3.87	3.16	3.32	0.00	3.32
WEST	3.60	3.87	3.61	3.32	4.00	2.65	3.87	3.46	3.12	0.00

Figure 8   Matrix of Social Role Distances Across Information and Money Exchange Networks

Omission of the redundant pairs need not be specified, and the distance equations above include the difference between z_{ijk} and z_{jik}. The examples in this monograph are based on so few cases that we felt the adjustment should be made here.

Figure 8 displays **D**, the distance matrix whose elements are the d_{ij}s between every pair of actors in both the information and money networks, calculated as in the preceding example. The two actors closest to each other are the Women's Rights Organization and the Westend neighborhood organization (d_{ij} = 2.65) and the two most distant pairs of actors are the chamber of commerce and education (4.24) and the mayor and the United Way (4.24). Because none of the ten actors has zero distance, imposing a strong structural equivalance criterion would result in no actors being placed together in the same network position. Measurement error, sampling variability, and other factors can conspire to render empirical network data less than perfectly reliable even for pairs of actors that are essentially equivalent in their ties to other system participants. For these reasons, a weak structural equivalence criterion is typically imposed to identify actor positions. To be placed together in the same positions, actors are required only to have a social distance equal to or less than some arbitrarily chosen nonzero value, α (alpha). That is,

$$d_{ij} \leqslant \alpha$$

Burt (1976, 1980), one of the most persistent proponents of the continuous distance approach to structural equivalence, selected values of alpha on the basis of a hierarchical clustering applied to the matrix of social role distances, **D**. *Cluster analysis* draws boundaries around objects in multidimensional space that result in maximal homogeneity (minimum variation) within each cluster (Bailey, 1974: 61). A hierarchical clustering may proceed by agglomeration: starting with N actors, the algorithm successively combines and recombines them into larger and larger clusters C, where $2 \leqslant C \leqslant N - 1$. Such clusters are mutually exclusive with regard to actor membership and nested at successive levels of aggregation. The most similar actors are joined in the early steps and the least similar actors join clusters only in the last steps. The result is a pattern resembling a *tree*: "A tree may be regarded as a hierarchical grouping structure, in which the objects in *B* are grouped into a set of clusters, these clusters are grouped into a set of clusters of clusters, and so on" (Hartigan, 1975: 1140). A tree can be diagramed as a *dendogram* to display the level of similarity at which actors and clusters merge into more inclusive clusters.

As applied to the matrix of social role distances, **D**, a hierarchical clustering sets the initial value of alpha at zero and combines into one cluster all actors with $d_{ij} = d_{ji} = 0$ (strong structural equivalence). In subsequent steps, the value of alpha is increased to successively higher levels found in the matrix **D**, combining the actors with these values into subsets that have greater similarity to each other than to other clusters. Successively greater values of alpha permit the clustering of clusters as structurally equivalent under more generous weak criteria until, at the final step, all actors are merged into a single group despite their separation by large social distances. At some intermediate point, the network researcher must select an arbitrary but reasonable alpha value that results in a partitioning of the N actors into a set of C clusters that will be the terminal set. No objective standard can be invoked as to the value of alpha at which clustering should be halted. Rather, the terminus must be selected by the researcher within the context of a substantive problem, guided by the uses to which the results are to be put and an inspection of the dendogram pattern of agglomeration.

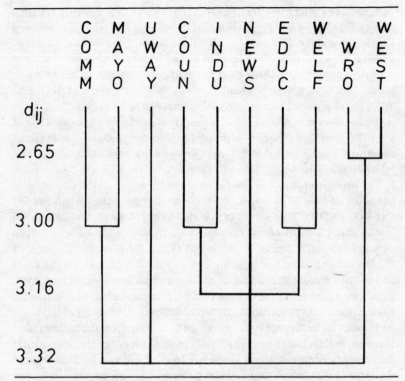

Figure 9   Dendogram Showing Hierarchical Clustering of Social Role Distance Matrix
in Figure 8

The result of applying a hierarchical clustering to the distance matrix in Figure 8 is displayed in the dendogram in Figure 9. This analysis was performed with the STRUCTURE program (Project, 1981), which uses Johnson's (1967) connectedness method of hierarchical clustering. After a cluster is formed, it is treated as a new object and its distance from the other objects is determined, with agglomeration at the next step based on the smallest distance between clusters (the alternative diameter method proceeds by using the largest distance). Westend and WRO are the first set of actors to be clustered (at alpha = 2.65). When alpha reaches 3.00, three new clusters emerge, each consisting of a pair of actors, while the newspaper and the United Way are the only isolates not yet joined with at least one other actor. If the network researcher decides to terminate the clustering at alpha = 3.16, three subsets would be identified (WRO, WEST), (COUN, INDU, NEWS, EDUC, WELF), and (COMM, MAYO), with a single isolate (UWAY). To proceed further would be futile, since all actors merge into a single hetero-geneous cluster at the next level of alpha.

Substantively, the three-cluster partitioning seems to make much sense. Both nonestablishment voluntary associations (WRO and WEST) are grouped together, based mainly on their absence of relations with the other actors. Indeed, this pair does not form a clique: None of the four possible exchanges of money and information occurs between them. According to Table 1, these two organizations are also the least influential actors, possibly as a consequence of their sparse connections in the two networks. The five-actor cluster consists of the city/county council and two of its bureaus, plus both private sector organizations (NEWS, INDU). This subset is internally structured much like a social circle: about a third of the forty possible dyadic relations across both networks actually occur. Finally, the two-actor cluster consisting of the mayor and chamber of commerce is almost a pure clique, as three of the four dyadic exchanges of money and information occur. Also, with a mean influence reputation of 5.83, it is somewhat more powerful than is the five-actor cluster (mean influence = 5.40; see Table 1).

Figure 10 rearranges the rows and columns of the money and information exchange network matrices to conform to the four-cluster partitioning obtained when alpha = 3.16. Vertical and horizontal lines demarcate the members of these clusters, as well as the single un-aggregated actor, UWAY. In the continuous distance approach, a *jointly occupied position* can be defined as a maximal set of structurally equivalent actors. A network position jointly occupied by three or more actors is called a *status*, S (Burt, 1980: 102). This minimum size requirement parallels the convention in clique detection. Under this definition, only a single status, S_1, exists in Figure 10. (In a system with a larger number of actors, presumably more statuses would be identi-fied.) The five actors COUN, INDU, NEWS, EDUC, and WELF jointly occupy this status because of their involvement in similar relational patterns with the actors across both networks.

The *role set* that defines a status is the mean or average of the rela-tions that link the status's occupants with each other and with the occupants of other statuses. In the kth network, the typical relation between a pair of positions, S_1 and S_2, jointly occupied by n_1 and n_2

Money

	COUN	INDU	NEWS	EDUC	WELF	COMM	MAYO	WRO	WEST	UWAY
COUN	0	0	0	1	1	0	1	0	1	1
INDU	0	0	1	1	1	1	0	0	0	1
NEWS	0	0	0	0	0	0	0	0	0	1
EDUC	0	0	0	0	0	0	0	0	0	1
WELF	0	0	0	1	0	0	0	0	0	1
COMM	0	0	0	1	0	0	0	0	0	0
MAYO	0	0	0	1	1	1	0	0	0	1
WRO	0	0	0	0	0	0	0	0	0	0
WEST	0	0	0	0	0	0	0	0	0	0
UWAY	0	0	0	0	1	0	0	0	1	0

Information

	COUN	INDU	NEWS	EDUC	WELF	COMM	MAYO	WRO	WEST	UWAY
COUN	0	0	1	0	1	1	1	0	0	0
INDU	1	0	1	0	0	1	1	0	0	0
NEWS	0	1	0	0	0	1	1	0	0	0
EDUC	0	1	1	0	0	1	1	1	1	0
WELF	0	0	1	0	0	1	1	0	0	0
COMM	1	1	1	1	1	0	1	0	0	1
MAYO	1	1	1	1	1	1	0	0	1	1
WRO	0	0	1	1	1	0	0	0	0	0
WEST	1	0	1	1	0	1	1	0	0	0
UWAY	1	1	1	0	1	1	1	0	0	0

Figure 10   Rearrangement of Money and Information Exchange

actors, respectively, is the mean or density of the ties from all occupants of S_1 to all members of S_2:

$$z_{12k} = \frac{\sum_{i=1}^{n_1} \sum_{q=1}^{n_2} z_{iqk}}{n_1 n_2}$$

while the average relation within-position S_1 is simply the density of ties among the position's occupants (ignoring self-ties in calculating the proportion):

$$z_{11k} = \frac{\sum_{i=1}^{n_1} \sum_{j=1}^{n_1} z_{ijk}}{n_1^2 - n_1}$$

where the ith and j^{th} actors occupy S_1 and the qth actor belongs to S_2.

Because only one status was found in the example data, we technically cannot compute the role set for S_1. However, for illustrative purposes, we shall consider the pair of two-actor clusters to constitute statuses S_2 and S_3. Then the role set defining S_1 is given by a ten-element vector consisting of five money and five information relations: (1) the mean relations from the occupants of S_1 to each of the other two statuses; (2) the mean relations to S_1 from each of the other two statuses; and (3) relations among the occupants of S_1. The full vector is:

$$(z_{12M} \; z_{13M} \; z_{21M} \; z_{31M} \; z_{11M} \; z_{12I} \; z_{13I} \; z_{21I} \; z_{31I} \; z_{11I})$$

which is, using the densities exhibited in Figure 10:

$$(0.2 \quad 0.1 \quad 0.3 \quad 0.0 \quad 0.3 \quad 1.0 \quad 0.2 \quad 1.0 \quad 0.6 \quad 0.4)$$

Similar role-set vectors of mean relations could be calculated for the network statuses S_2 and S_3. The concept of network status will be used below in discussing hypothesis testing.

One advantage to the continuous distance approach to structural equivalence is the ability to represent actors' relations visually in a manner analogous to the sociogram of direct linkages described above. The matrix of Euclidean distances between actors, **D**, can be entered in any of a variety of multidimensional scaling programs (Kruskal and Wish, 1978), and a geometric display of social space will be produced in d dimensions (d < N), along with a measure of fit between the data and the configuration. In Figure 11, we show the results of a two-dimensional smallest space analysis (Roskam and Lingoes, 1970; McFarland and Brown, 1973) based on input of the distances in Figure 8. The stress coefficient is 0.11, an acceptable value. We have drawn closed curves around the three clusters of actors identified in Figure 10. The diagram clearly shows dispersion of actors and positions across the social space underlying the two exchange networks, with a noted tendency for each actor's location to reflect its influence reputation (the linear correlations of the influence scores in Figure 3 are -.45 and -.67 with SSA dimensions one and two, respectively).

DISCRETE DISTANCE

A second approach to structural equivalence partitioning of network matrices is the *blockmodel* method introduced by White and his colleagues (Breiger et al., 1975; White et al., 1976; Boorman and White, 1976; Arabie et al., 1978; Arabie and Boorman, 1981). Blockmodeling involves both a procedure for grouping actors into structurally equivalent position (blocks) and a technique for analyzing the role structure of multiple relations among the blocks. This subsection concentrates on the blocking methodology and defers until later a consideration of the role algebra component of blockmodeling.

The most widely used algorithm for partitioning multiple network matrices is CONCOR (CONvergence of iterated CORrelations), a hierarchical clustering procedure that starts with a set of K observed matrices. The matrices, each representing a distinct network of relations among N actors, are "stacked" to create a single KN × N matrix for input into a correlation program. The program first calculates the Pearson product-moment correlation coefficients (r_{ij}) between every pair of columns (i.e., between every pair of actors). The resulting N × N matrix of correlations, **R**, thus contains linear measures of similarity between every pair of actors, based on their ties from all other actors. The larger the positive correlation, the greater the structural equivalence of a pair.

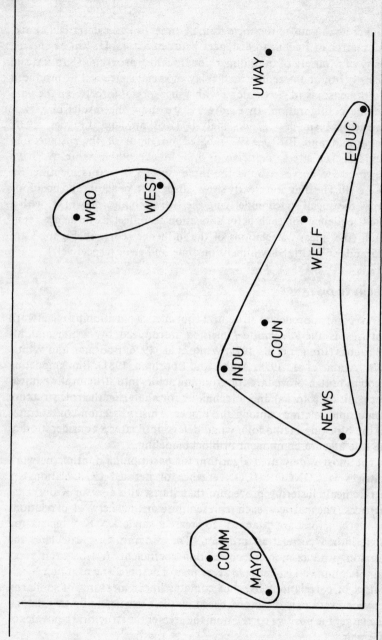

Figure 11 Smallest Space Analysis of Distances in Figure 6

In the next step, CONCOR submits the **R** matrix itself to the correlation program, this time correlating all pairs of columns (each column consisting of N correlation coefficients). The resulting matrix of second-order correlations is likewise fed back into the correlation program, and the process is repeated until all entries in **R** are either +1.0 or –1.0. The final result is a two-block partitioning of the original set of network actors, with all actors positively correlated belonging to one block and all actors negatively correlated with members of that block belonging to the second block. The CONCOR algorithm may then be repeated separately on each subset, producing additional bipartitions. The cycle can continue until every actor is placed in its own block (N-block partition). Thus, CONCOR is a hierarchical clustering program based on successively dividing the entire network into smaller and smaller blocks, in diametrical contrast to the continuous distance approach that agglomerates individual actors into successively larger clusters. Both procedures require the network researcher to make a substantive decision about where to halt the lumping or splitting.

CONCOR calculates correlations using the columns of the K stacked matrices, that is, on the set of relations received from all system actors across all K networks. Alternatively, iterative correlations could be calculated using the row vectors (i.e., the set of all ties sent to other actors). A third possibility is to use both the ties sent and the ties received, by including the K transposed matrices in the set of stacked input data. (A transposed matrix is one in which the z_{ij} and z_{ji} elements are exchanged. See Schwartz, 1977, for an argument that all diagonal elements should be excluded in computing correlations in CONCOR.) Because our illustration above of the continuous distance approach calculated Euclidean distances on both rows and columns, the following CONCOR example will also be based on both relations sent and received in the money and information exchange matrices.

To return to the same dyad discussed before, the correlation between the United Way and the welfare department using the forty paired binary values is .26, indicating a modest level of similarity in these two organizations' patterns of relations with other system actors. Figure 12 displays the full matrix of correlations among the ten organizations produced in the first CONCOR step. A comparison with the values reported in the social distance matrix (Figure 8) indicates a high degree of inverse covariation (high r_{ij} with low d_{ij}, and vice versa), but not a simple linear transformation of values. The correlation of the 45 non-diagonal distance values in the **D** matrix with the corresponding correlations in the **R** matrix is –.84.

R

	COUN	COMM	EDUC	INDU	MAYO	WRO	NEWS	UWAY	WELF	WEST
COUN	1.00	.14	.15	.45	.28	.10	.30	.26	.34	.11
COMM	.14	1.00	−.06	.14	.40	.35	.30	.14	.14	.21
EDUC	.15	−.06	1.00	.04	−.04	−.10	.32	.38	.47	.17
INDU	.45	.14	.04	1.00	.38	.10	.30	.15	.34	.36
MAYO	.28	.40	−.04	.38	1.00	.32	.32	−.04	.07	.15
WRO	.10	.35	−.10	.10	.32	1.00	−.09	.07	−.07	.42
NEWS	.30	.30	.32	.30	.32	−.09	1.00	.00	.41	.08
UWAY	.26	.14	.38	.15	−.04	.07	.00	1.00	.26	.29
WELF	.34	.14	.47	.34	.07	−.07	.41	.26	1.00	.36
WEST	.11	.21	.17	.36	.15	.42	.08	.29	.36	1.00

Figure 12 Matrix of Column and Row Correlations Across Information and Money Exchange Networks

The contrast between the continuous and discrete distance algorithms is facilitated by comparing the ways that correlations and distances are computed on binary data. Consider the standard 2×2 layout with cell and marginal frequences indicated by letters:

		Y		
		0	1	Total
X	1	a	b	a + b
	0	c	d	c + d
	Total	a + c	b + d	a + b + c + d

The formula for the Pearson correlation is simply that for the non-parametric statistic phi:

$$r_{ij} = \frac{bc - ad}{\sqrt{(a + b)(c + d)(b + d)(a + c)}}$$

The Euclidean distance formula boils down to:

$$d_{ij} = \sqrt{a + d}$$

Thus distance and correlation are not simply linear transformations of one another. Distance is always nonnegative, while correlations vary on a standardized scale from -1 to $+1$. Given those differences in the basic similarity measures, a substantive difference in the identification of positions and their occupants is understandable.

Proceeding with the CONCOR analysis, convergence to the ± 1.0 matrix occurred on the tenth iteration. One block consisted of COMM, MAYO, WRO, and WEST, and the other block's members were COUN, INDU, NEWS, EDUC, UWAY, and WELF. Subsequent partitions of both blocks resulted in the following four-block assignments:

(1) COMM, MAYO
(2) WRO, WEST
(3) COUN, INDU, NEWS
(4) EDUC, UWAY, WELF

This partition bears some resemblance to the continuous distance clusterings above, except that EDUC and WELF have been split off the third block and placed in a position with UWAY. These differences underscore the fact that the two methods operationalize structural equivalence somewhat differently and approach hierarchical clustering in a different fashion.

The main distinction, however, between the discrete and continuous distance methods lies in their assumptions about space. CONCOR produces a classification of network actors into discrete, mutually exclusive and exhaustive categories. It obtains neither measures of proximity between blocks nor even an intrinsic ordered relation among the blocks. Thus, their numbering from 1 to 4 is arbitrary. In contrast, the continuous distance method preserves Euclidean distances during its aggregation of actors into jointly occupied positions. Retaining the metric permits the application of powerful statistical methods testing hypotheses, as discussed below. For further observations on the basic spatial assumptions of the two approaches to structural equivalence, see Burt (1977a: 125-127).

CONCOR, like the continuous distance approach, is an algorithm that searches for structurally equivalent sets of actors, useful where no strong a priori hypothesis exists about network structure. The CONCOR algorithm is not a validated procedure: There is no proof of the invariant convergence to the ± 1.0 matrix form, and it is unclear what objective function (if any) is minimized or maximized by the process (Schwartz, 1977). Nonetheless, CONCOR has been found repeatedly to be "empirically useful in producing interpretable block-models" (Arabie and Boorman, 1982), and for that reason its popularity remains high.

Matrix Permutation and Images

After the network actors have been partitioned into subsets of structurally equivalent positions, the original data matrices can be permuted to reveal the underlying intra- and interpositional relations. *Permutation* is a rearrangement of corresponding rows and columns to bring together in adjacent portions of each network matrix those actors that jointly occupy the same position or block. Vertical and horizontal lines can be drawn at appropriate places in the permuted matrices to show the distinct positions identified by the hierarchical clustering. This rearrangement is essentially the same manipulation described above for the results of the continuous distance approach. Figure 13a shows the money exchange matrix permuted according to both two- and four-block partitioning resulting from the CONCOR analysis of the money, information, and their two transposed matrices. The comparable permutation of the information matrix is not shown. Note again that the sequence of blocks and of actors within blocks is entirely arbitrary, as CONCOR imposes no order among positions.

After permutation, the original matrix may be reduced to its image. An *image matrix* is obtained from a blocked matrix by replacing each of its submatrices by either a 0 or a 1 according to the density of relations within each submatrix. Typically, one of two density criteria is used: (1) submatrices with no ties among actors are coded 0s (*zero-blocks*) and submatrices with one or more ties are coded as 1s (*one-blocks*), or (2) some *cutoff density* value, alpha, is chosen at the researcher's discretion and all submatrices with densities less than alpha are set to 0, while all submatrices with alpha density and above are set to 1. (A frequently imposed cutoff density is the grand density for the matrix as a whole.) The first criterion is extremely restrictive in requiring zero-

A. Permuted and Blocked Matrix

M	C O M M	M A Y O	W R O	W E S T	C O U N	I N D U	N E W S	E D U C	U W A Y	W E L F
COMM	–	0	0	0	0	0	0	1	0	0
MAYO	1	–	0	0	0	0	0	1	1	1
WRO	0	0	–	0	0	0	0	0	0	0
WEST	0	0	0	–	0	0	0	0	0	0
COUN	0	1	0	1	–	0	0	1	1	1
INDU	1	0	0	0	0	–	1	1	1	1
NEWS	1	0	0	0	0	0	–	0	1	0
EDUC	0	0	0	0	0	0	0	–	1	0
UWAY	0	0	0	1	0	0	0	0	–	1
WELF	0	0	0	0	0	0	0	1	1	–

B. Block Densities

	1-2	3-4
1-2	.09	.17
3-4	.21	.40

C. Block Image

	1-2	3-4
1-2	0	0
3-4	0	1

Figure 13   Permuted Money Exchange Matrix with Two-Block Densities and Image Matrix

blocks to be strictly filled with 0s, probably an unrealistic assumption for fallible social data. Using a higher cutoff density to decide which submatrices will be coded 0 and 1 in the image matrix is usually more realistic and substantively revealing. The more liberal criterion tolerates a few ties between dyads across what are essentially unrelated positions.

The abstraction of an image from a blocked matrix is a *homomorphism* of the observed relations, that is, a mapping from a blocked matrix to an image matrix that maps one-blocks to 1s and zero-blocks to 0s (Arabie et al., 1978; this use of homomorphism is not to be con-

Two-Block Images

	Money			Information	
	1-2	3-4		1-2	3-4
1-2	0	0		0	1
3-4	0	1		1	0

Four-Block Images

	Money					Information			
	1	2	3	4		1	2	3	4
1	1	0	0	1		1	0	1	1
2	0	0	0	0		0	0	0	0
3	1	0	0	1		1	0	1	0
4	0	0	0	1		1	0	1	0

Figure 14   Two- and Four-Block Images of Money and Information Exchange
Networks

fused with the semigroup homomorphism developed by Boorman and
White, 1976). The homomorphic reduction of the two-block partition
of the money exchange network to its image is illustrated in Figure 13.
Figure 13b shows densities for the four submatrices or positions
(density calculations exclude the main diagonals, since self-ties were
prohibited in the data). As mentioned above, the mean density for the
entire matrix is 0.24. Only one of the four submatrices exceeds this
cutoff value, and thus the other three submatrices are set to zero, as
shown in Figure 13c. The resulting two-block money exchange image
matrix thus reveals that money flows only from the second position
to the second position. This position is not a true clique, however, since
its density is not 1.00, which would indicate a maximal complete
subgraph.

In Figure 14, we display the two-block and four-block images for
both the money and information exchange networks, again using the
mean density cutoff criterion for each full matrix. At the simpler two-

block level, information trading between the two positions is apparent: The highest densities occurred in the submatrices involving information exchanges between sets of actors occupying different positions. In the more refined four-block partition, a more complex pair of images emerges. Several genuine zero-blocks are encountered, eight in the money and two in the information networks. And all five one-blocks in the information network that involve the first position have densities of 1.00. The most obvious consistency across both networks is the absence of connection between position 2, consisting of the two non-establishment associations WRO and WEST, with any other position, including themselves. This position is completely isolated from a sustained relation with any other positions. In the money exchange image, position 4 (EDUC, UWAY, WELF) is the main recipient of money transactions, receiving support from the other two positions as well as from its own members. Position 3 (COUN, INDU, NEWS) does not receive funds from any subset of network members, but it does supply both position 4 and position 1 (COMM, MAYO), which also provides some of its own financial support.

In the information exchange matrix positions 1 and 3 are the main recipients, from all sources (including within their own positions) except for the isolated position 2. Position 4 is differentiated in receiving community affairs information only from the first position, in striking contrast to its role as a financial recipient in the other network.

Hypothesis Testing

The techniques for analyzing relations among multiple networks of actors presented above are primarily descriptive. The procedures would be more valuable if network researchers could formulate and test hypotheses about the social structures observed in the data. Unfortunately, statistical tests are not available for clique models. The restrictive definition of a clique as three or more actors that form a maximal complete subgraph is a condition either met or not met by an empirical network, and hence no significance test is feasible. Definitions of less stringent cliquelike subgroups are just too nebulous to provide a baseline for testing the degree to which subsets of empirical actors conform to these cliquelike structures. Only when cliques are defined as structurally equivalent actors also tied to each other by a strong criterion (alpha = 0) can cliques be treated to statistical tests as a special case of a jointly occupied position, as described next.

Hypotheses about the triad combinations in networks can be subjected to statistical tests, using the triad census, a vector of sixteen types of triads that can occur in network data. Description of the test statistic would require too much space, so the interested reader is advised to consult Holland and Leinhardt (1975 and 1978). An even more mathematically arcane approach is the biased nets model for assessing deviations from randomness in relations among actors (Rapoport and Horvath, 1961).

Burt (1976, 1977a, 1977b, 1980) developed factor-analytic procedures for testing a center-periphery hypothesis about the distances of structurally equivalent actors from a status position represented as a single point in space. Page limitations allow us only to sketch the general outlines of the test.

Using structural equivalence methods described above to compute the distances among the N actors in a multiple network system, subsets of actors are hierarchically clustered into distinct statuses, S, each containing three or more actors. For the K actors jointly occupying status position S_k, we observe only the $K^2 - K$ distances between pairs of actors (the d_{ij}). Under the hypothesis to be tested, a single unobserved vector of true distances from a single point in the status to each actor is responsible for (i.e., "causes") the observed variation in these d_{ij} interactor distances. Thus, the empirical distances among the structurally equivalent actors jointly occupying a status may be treated as fallible indicators of the true vector.

The situation is depicted in path diagrammatic terms in Figure 15. At the top, the unobserved status S_k is represented as producing variation in the distance of each actor (d_i) from the center point of the status. The path coefficients (λ_{ik}) from S_k to the d_is reflect the different role distances of each of the K actors, with larger values of λ_{ik} indicating greater proximity to the center and smaller values reflecting greater distance.

Because the relations may be measured with random error, an actor's distance from the center of the status is shown also to be affected by a random error component (δ_i), whose effect (Θ_i) indicates the degree to

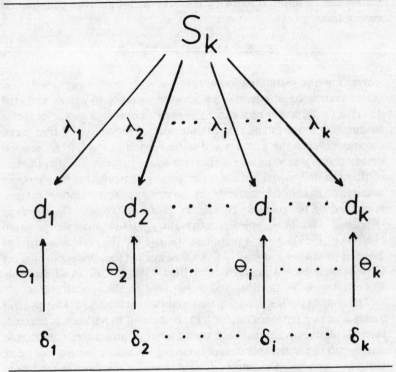

Figure 15 Path Diagram of Covariance Structure for the Center-Periphery
Hypothesis

which the relations in which actor i are involved is an accurate indicator
of the role set defining status S_k. Under this restricted covariance structure for the center-periphery hypothesis, the observed covariance between any pair of occupants of a status is equal to the product of their
λ_{ik} coefficients, indicating the extent to which their relational patterns
reflect the status's role set. If the center-periphery hypothesis is correct,
then the covariance structure depicted in Figure 15 will accurately
describe the observed covariance matrix among the distances of the
K actors (the covariance matrix of the d_{ij}s).

The K $\times$ K observed variance/covariance, $\mathbf{S}$ (not to be confused with
S_k, the kth status), is estimated from the observed distances. This $\mathbf{S}$

matrix can be approximated by the basic factor analytic equation, in matrix form:

$$S = \Sigma = \Lambda\Phi\Lambda' + \Theta_\delta^2 = \Lambda\Lambda' + \Theta_\delta^2$$

where Σ is the estimated variance/covariance matrix, Λ is a $1 \times K$ vector composed of covariances between distance to actors and true distance to the center of status S_k to each actor (i.e., a vector of factor loadings); Φ is the (standardized) variance of the vector of true social distance between the K actors and status S_k; and Θ_Δ^2 is a $K \times K$ diagonal matrix containing variances of the error scores in the vector. Parameters of the specified model are estimated through principal components or maximum likelihood methods by submitting a correlation matrix, computed on the pairwise correlation of the columns of the observed interactor distances, to a confirmatory factor analysis program (Jöreskog, 1969). A chi-square test statistic for the goodness of fit of Σ to S is produced and may be evaluated against the appropriate degree of freedom in estimating the model (Burt, 1980: 109, notes adjustments to both degrees of freedom and χ^2 required by the specification).

The null hypothesis asserts that actors in status S_k are equivalent under a strong criterion (alpha = 0). If the null hypothesis is rejected, then S_k defines a status only under a weak structural equivalence criterion. That is, the role distances among the actors jointly occupying the status S_k are significantly different from 0, but still small relative to other network actors not in the status.

Under a weak structural equivalence criterion, a jointly occupied status is not defined by a single point but as a field surrounding a point in multidimensional space. To test hypotheses about distance as a point in space, two or more of the status occupants must be specified as indicators of the role distance to the status. In this more typical situation, the standardized values of the λ_i express the correlation between actors' role distances to the status as defined in terms of its indicator actors and the role distance to the observed position of each actor. Actors on the periphery of a status (i.e., those incorporated into a position under larger alpha values during the hierarchical clustering) will have lower covariation with distance to the status than will the core actors.

Hypothesis testing for blockmodels based on discrete distance between positions in multiple networks has not been fully developed to date. BLOCKER, a computer program for finding simultaneous homomorphic correspondences between binarized matrices and images (Heil and White, 1976), allows an investigator to specify as input a set of hypothesized images on the basis of some theoretical considerations. The program then looks at all possible permutations of the original matrices involving a "lean fit" (pure zero-blocks) that could fit the hypothesized blocking. The number of blocks and a lower bound on block size may be specified by the user. The program has been useful in identifying "floaters," actors whose block membership is ambiguous, and who thus could be assigned to two or more different blocks without violating the hypothesis. In practice, BLOCKER has fallen into disfavor because it requires a network researcher to have a priori knowledge of the data structure and it tolerates no impurities in zero-blocks. The inductive CONCOR algorithm avoids both these rigorous requirements and has been more favored in practice as the mean to identify blocks and their occupants. Still, BLOCKER serves the important function of forcing the network analyst to think clearly about the specific structural patterns that are theoretically expected. Properly used, this procedure could make important contributions to tightening the link between theory and data in network research.

Goodness-of-fit tests for proposed blockmodels have been suggested by White (1977), Carrington et al. (1980), Carrington and Heil (1981), and Morgan and Wolfarth (1980), although they have yet to see wide acceptance. The underlying idea is to compare a proposed blocked binary matrix or matrices with the matrix that would be expected under a null hypothesis, using either correlations or a chi-square statistic as the measure of association. Several of these techniques have severe constraints on the types of data to which they can be applied and have unknown distributional properties that do not permit legitimate tests of statistical significance. And in some cases, the hypothesized comparison model is trivial, e.g., a matrix of random relations, whose rejection adds little to what is already known about the data structure. Clearly, statistics for testing blockmodel hypotheses is an area of network research greatly in need of much development.

Another topic needing further development is the relative importance of various network relations in multiple network analyses. When several matrices are used jointly in partitioning a set of actors into subgroups, their differential densities can affect the clustering results. At present, adequate criteria have not been developed for determining the degree of redundancy among multiple network relations or for assessing the unique contributions among a set of matrices in producing a joint partition. Weighting effects in structural equivalence procedures is an important topic for future research.

Analysis of Structural Correlates

The preceding sections of this chapter discussed at length some procedures for investigating two fundamental components of network analysis. This first component consists of means for detecting network structures, such as cliques and structurally equivalent positions, by partitioning a relational matrix into subgroups. The second component involves characterizing actors, subgroups, or complete networks in various structural terms, such as centrality, prestige, connectedness, multiplexity, density, and the like. Upon completion of these preliminary tasks, a network researcher may apply a third component of network analysis, which may be called the analysis of homophyly or, more simply, of structural correlates.

The basis question addressed by these procedures is: What are the causes, concomitants, or consequences of social structure for actors, subgroups, or complete networks? For example, after dividing a network of community elites into subgroups based on the patterns of community affairs discussions, a political sociologist may wish to determine the extent to which these structurally equivalent positions are ideologically homogeneous. Given some measure of individuals' political ideologies, an appropriate test might be an analysis of variance using the groups as the treatment variable. A significant F ratio would indicate that the positions vary in their mean political views, the correlation ratio would reveal how strongly structural position predicts the elite individuals' ideologies, and the effect coefficients would show which groups are above and below the mean on the ideology scale.

Attribute data could be combined with relational measures in a general linear model. Thus known or hypothesized variables such as elites' ages, incomes, and party affiliations could be entered into a regression equation along with a set of dummy variables reflecting position membership and the net effects of each predictor variable on the political ideology scale could be estimated by ordinary least squares procedures. For examples of such combined attribute-relation analyses see Breiger (1976) and Mullins et al. (1977) on natural scientists, Galaskiewicz (1979) and Knoke (forthcoming) on community organizations, and Snyder and Kick (1979) on the world system of nation-states.

Laumann et al. (1974) demonstrated another approach to combining relational and attribute data. They developed a causal model in which the units of analysis were not individual actors but the $(N^2 - N)/2$ interpoint distances between pairs of elites in a small German town's community discussion network. These distances were derived from a smallest space solution to a matrix of path distances. Antecedent variables in their path model were measures of the similarity/dissimilarity of the actor pairs on such factors as religion, party affiliation, and sociopolitical values. The substantive conclusion was that proximity within the community affairs discussion network was most strongly affected by social ties between the actor pairs (see Laumann et al., 1977, for a comparison of findings for two American cities).

Other variations on the structural correlates theme include ego-alter strategies (e.g., Duncan et al.'s 1968 analysis of occupational aspirations of pairs of high school students; see also Coleman et al.'s 1966 classic study of medical innovation diffusion) and geographic space analysis (Doreian, 1981). The analysis of structural correlates is still in the preliminary stage and the years ahead will likely see a rapid proliferation of new approaches and formal analyses of their methodological properties.

Other Issues

We have not begun to exhaust the wide variety of methodological topics in network analysis. Unfortunately, space limitations permit only a cursory overview of other issues, some of which are still in the developmental stage.

Clustering. With exceptionally large data sets—for example, more than 500 actors or more than 20 distinct networks—conventional partitioning methods such as CONCOR may be inefficient and costly. Adaptation of alternative clustering algorithms, such as the K-means approach (MacQueen, 1967; Hartigan and Wong, 1979) or a combinatorial approach (see Arabie and Boorman, 1982), may provide a better solution for clustering actors into subsets.

The discrete and continuous distance methods for clustering structurally equivalent actors both result in hierarchical partitionings of the networks. That is, mutually exclusive equivalence classes of actors are identified simultaneously across all K networks, as shown by a dendogram or tree diagram. However, such restrictions are often conceptually unrealistic, as actors may belong to more than one social group (e.g., may participate in several social circles, formal organizations, familial segments, and so on). Thus, nonhierarchical procedures that allow overlapping clusters to emerge can provide an alternative approach (Arabie, 1982). The recently developed MAPCLUS (Mathematical Programming Clustering) algorithm (Arabie and Carroll, 1980) allows the user to specify the number of subsets in the final solution and does not restrict subsets to be maximal complete subgraphs.

Structural Relatedness. The structural equivalence concept identifies actors jointly occupying a social position on the basis of similar relations to the *same* other network actors. An alternative conceptualization of social roles argues that actors should occupy the same role to the extent that they maintain relations to *equivalent* other network actors. For example, a set of foremen supervises different workers, a set of fathers disciplines different children, and a set of professors teaches different students. Thus two actors in a network are structurally related if they are connected in the same or similar ways to structurally related actors (Sailer, 1978). This reconceptualization of social role requires a different algorithm than the blockmodel or continuous distance procedures to locate structurally related actors (see Mandel and Winship, 1981). White and Reitz (1982) provided a useful overview of these issues.

Role Algebra. As developed by White and his colleagues (Lorrain and White, 1971; Boorman and White, 1976), blockmodeling involves more than the clustering technique described above. The structural regularities among positions, as represented in the binary image matrices, could be uncovered by the set of indirect or compound relations formed from all the direct relations for the K networks. The technical details of this role algebra are too complex to present in this monograph, so the interested reader is referred to the original articles, as well as to modifications proposed by Bonacich (1980; also Bonacich and McConaghy, 1979; Breiger and Pattison, 1978; McConaghy, 1981).

Change over Time. The methods and examples discussed in this monograph all refer to data collected on networks observed at a single point in time. Dynamic methods for modeling changing relations are just coming to the attention of social researchers (Wasserman, 1979, 1980; Runger and Wasserman, 1980; Galaskiewicz and Wasserman, 1981). These models are based on continuous-time or discrete-time Markov chains that enable a researcher to estimate parameters describing the rates of formation or disappearance of linkages in the networks. As with many aspects of network research, the methodological sophistication in this area seems to have run ahead of the theoretical and substantive developments that could take advantage of the methods.

Microstructure. Another complex network methodology whose exposition cannot be encompassed within the present space is the analysis of local structures. In a network of N actors, there are $(N^3 - 3N + 2N)/6$ possible triads of actors, but only sixteen unique triad structures involving mutual strong, asymmetric, or mutual null ties between pairs. Various theoretical models—balance, cluster, ranked cluster, and transitivity—make predictions about the permissibility of various triads (see Leik and Meeker, 1975: 53-74). The research program of Davis, Holland, and Leinhardt (Davis, 1979) made substantial progress in specifying and testing various aspects of such models on triad data (see Holland and Leinhardt, 1970, 1975, 1978; Davis and Leinhardt, 1972, for some basic results). Microstructural analyses describe relations among individual actors. Still unresolved is the question of how such local structures contribute to structures observed at the total network level of analysis.

Computer Programs. Finally, construction and maintenance of a data file for relational and attribute data can be a complex and time-consuming task. Although every network researcher will discover unique elements to be incorporated for specific objectives, some features will be common to most research projects, especially the ability to rapidly assemble matrices, collapse or reduce the rows and columns, symmetrize entries, and multiply and add matrix elements. Roistacher (1979) and Sonquist (1980; see also Mulherin et al., 1981) offer useful suggestions for organizing network data files. Sonquist (1980) also provides a census of 28 computer programs for various types of network analyses, including information on the machines and computer languages in which they were originally written, as well as references for locating further details. Many designers make their programs and manuals available at the nominal cost of materials and postage. Readers are advised to consult recent issues of the journals *Social Networks* and *Connections* for updated listings of new programs.

REFERENCES

ALBA, R. D. (1973) "A graph-theoretic definition of a sociometric clique." Journal of Mathematical Sociology 3: 113-126.

——— and C. KADUSHIN (1976) "The intersection of social circles: a new measure of social proximity in networks." Sociological Methods & Research 5: 77-102.

ALBA, R. D. and G. MOORE (1978) "Elite social circles." Sociological Methods & Research 7: 167-188.

ALLEN, M. P. (1974) "The structure of interorganizational elite cooptation: interlocking corporate directors." American Sociological Review 39: 393-406.

ANDERSON, B. (1979) "Cognitive balance theory and social network analysis: remarks on some fundamental theoretical matters," pp. 453-469 in Paul W. Holland and Samuel Leinhardt (eds.) Perspectives on Social Network Research. New York: Academic.

ARABIE, P. (1982) "Conceptions of overlap in social structure," in L. Freeman, A. K. Romney, and D. R. White (eds.) Methods of Social Network Analysis.

——— and S. BOORMAN (1982) "Blockmodels: developments and prospects," in H. Hudson (ed.) Classifying Social Data: New Applications of Analytic Methods for Social Science Research. San Francisco: Jossey-Bass.

——— and P. R. LEVITT (1978) "Constructing blockmodels: how and why." Journal of Mathematical Psychology 17: 21-63.

ARABIE, P. and J. D. CARROLL (1980) "MAPPLUS: a mathematical programming approach to fitting the ADCLUS model." Psychometrika 45: 211-235.

ATKIN, R. H. (1977) Combinatorial Connectivities in Social Systems: An Application of Simplicial Complex Structures to the Study of Large Organizations. Basel: Birkhauser Verlag.

——— (1974) Mathematical Structure in Human Affairs. London: Heinemann.

AUGUSTSON, J. G. and J. MINKER (1970) "An analysis of some graph theoretical cluster techniques." Journal of the ACM 17: 571-588.

BAILEY, K. (1974) "Cluster analysis," pp. 59-128 in D. R. Heise (ed.) Sociological Methodology 1975. San Francisco: Jossey-Bass.

BARNES, J. A. (1979) "Network analysis: orienting notion, rigorous technique or substantive field of study?" pp. 403-423 in Paul Holland and Samuel Leinhardt (eds.) Perspectives on Social Network Research. New York: Academic.

BAVELAS, A. (1950) "Communication patterns in task oriented groups." Journal of the Acoustical Society of America 22: 271-282.

BEHZAD, M. and G. CHARTRAND (1971) Introduction to the Theory of Graphs. Boston: Allyn & Bacon.

BENIGER, J. R. (1976) "Sampling social networks: the subgroup approach." Proceedings of the Business and Economic Statistics Section, American Statistical Association: 226-231.

BERNARD, H. R. and P. D. KILLWORTH (1978) "A review of the small-world literature." Connections 2: 15-24.

——— (1977) "Informant accuracy in social network data II." Human Communication Research 4: 3-18.

—————— and L. SAILER (1980) "Informant accuracy in social network data IV: a comparison of clique-level structure in behavioral and cognitive network data." Social Networks 2: 191-218.

BOISSEVAIN, J. (1974) Friends of Friends: Networks, Manipulators, and Coalitions. New York: St. Martin's.

BONACICH, P. (1980) "The 'common structure,' a replacement for the Boorman and White 'joint reduction'." American Journal of Sociology 86: 159-166.

—————— and M. J. McCONAGHY (1979) "The algebra of blockmodeling," pp. 489-532 in K. F. Schuessler (ed.) Sociological Methodology 1980. San Francisco: Jossey-Bass.

BOORMAN, S. A. and H. C. WHITE (1976) "Social structure from multiple networks. II. role structures." American Journal of Sociology 81: 1384-1446.

BOTT, E. (1955) "Urban families: conjugal roles and social networks." Human Relations 8: 345-383.

BREIGER, R. L. (1976) "Career attributes and network structure: a blockmodel study of a biomedical research specialty." American Sociological Review 41: 117-135.

—————— (1974) "The duality of persons and groups." Social Forces 53: 181-190.

—————— S. A. BOORMAN, and P. ARABIE (1975) "An algorithm for clustering relational data, with applications to social network analysis and comparison with multidimensional scaling." Journal of Mathematical Psychology 12: 328-383.

BREIGER, R. L. and P. E. PATTISON (1978) "The joint role structure of two communities' elites." Sociological Methods & Research 7: 213-226.

BURT, R. S. (1982) Toward a Structural Theory of Action: Network Models of Social Structure, Perceptions and Action. New York: Academic.

—————— (1981) "Studying status/role-sets as ersatz network positions in mass surveys." Sociological Methods & Research 9: 313-337.

—————— (1980) "Models of network structure." Annual Review of Sociology 6: 79-141.

—————— (1979) "A structural theory of interlocking corporate directorates." Social Networks 1: 415-435.

—————— (1978) "Cohesion versus structural equivalence as a basis for network subgroups." Sociological Methods & Research 7: 189-212.

—————— (1977a) "Positions in multiple network systems. Part one: a general conception of stratification and prestige in a system of actors cast as a social typology." Social Forces 57: 106-131.

—————— (1977b) "Positions in multiple network systems. Part two: stratification and prestige among elite decision-makers in the community of Altneustadt." Social Forces 56: 551-575.

—————— (1976) "Positions in networks." Social Forces 55: 93-122.

—————— (1975) "Corporate society: a time series analysis of network structure." Social Science Research 4: 271-328.

—————— and W. M. BITTNER (1981) "A note on inferences regarding network subgroups." Social Networks 3: 71-83.

BURT, R. S., K. P. CHRISTMAN, and H. C. KILBURN, Jr. (1980) "Testing a structural theory of corporate cooptation: interorganizational directorate ties as a strategy for avoiding market constraints on profits." American Sociological Review 45: 821-841.

BURT, R. S. and N. LIN (1977) "Network time series from archival records," pp. 224-254 in D. R. Heise (ed.) Sociological Methodology 1977. San Francisco: Jossey-Bass.

CAPOBIANCO, M. F. (1970) "Statistical inference in finite populations having structure." Transactions of the New York Academy of Sciences 32: 401-413.

CARRINGTON, P. J. and G. H. HEIL (1981) "COBLOC: a hierarchical method for blocking network data." Journal of Mathematical Sociology 8: 103-131.

——— and S. D. BERKOWITZ (1980) "A goodness-of-fit index for blockmodels." Social Networks 2: 219-234.

CARTWRIGHT, D. and F. HARARY (1956) "Structural balance: a generalization of Heider's theory." Psychological Review 63: 277-292.

COLEMAN, J. S., E. KATZ, and H. MENZEL (1966) Medical Innovation: A Diffusion Study. Indianapolis: Bobbs-Merrill.

COLEMAN, J. S. and D. MacRAE, Jr. (1960) "Electronic processing of sociometric data for groups up to 1000 in size." American Sociological Review 25: 722-727.

COOK, K. S. and R. M. EMERSON (1978) "Power, equity and commitment in exchange networks." American Sociological Review 43: 721-739.

CRANE, D. (1969) "Social structure in a group of scientists: a test of the 'invisible college' hypothesis." American Sociological Review 34: 335-352.

DAVIS, J. A. (1979) "The Davis/Holland/Leinhardt studies: an overview," pp. 51-62 in P. W. Holland and S. Leinhardt (eds.) Perspectives on Social Network Research. New York: Academic.

——— and S. LEINHARDT (1972) "The structure of positive interpersonal relations in small groups," pp. 218-251 in J. Berger (ed.) Sociological Theories in Progress, Vol. 2. Boston: Houghton-Mifflin.

DOREIAN, P. (1981) "On the estimation of linear models with spatially distributed data," pp. 359-388 in Samuel Leinhardt (ed.) Sociological Methodology 1981. San Francisco: Jossey-Bass.

——— (1980) "On the evolution of group network structure." Social Networks 2: 235-254.

——— (1969) "A note on the detection of cliques in valued graphs." Sociometry 32: 237-242.

DUFFIN, R. J., E. L. PETERSON, and C. ZENER (1967) Geometric Programming. New York: John Wiley.

DUNCAN, O. D., A. O. HALLER, and A. PORTES (1968) "Peer influences on aspirations: a reinterpretation." American Journal of Sociology 74: 119-137.

ERICKSON, B. H., T. A. NOSANCHUK, and E. LEE (1981) "Network sampling in practice: some second steps." Social Networks 3: 127-136.

EULAU, H. (1980) "The Columbia studies of personal influence." Social Science History 4: 207-228.

FESTINGER, L. (1949) "The analysis of sociograms using matrix algebra." Human Relations 2: 153-158.

FISCHER, C. S. (1982) To Dwell Among Friends: Personal Networks in Town and City. Chicago: University of Chicago Press.

FLAMENT, C. (1963) Applications of Graph Theory to Group Structure. Englewood Cliffs, NJ: Prentice-Hall.

FORSYTH, E. and L. KATZ (1946) "A matrix approach to the analysis of sociometric data: preliminary report." Sociometry 9: 340-347.

FRANK, O. (1979) "Estimation of population totals by use of snowball samples," pp. 319-347 in Paul W. Holland and Samuel Leinhardt (eds.) Perspectives on Social Network Research. New York: Academic.

––––– (1978) "Sampling and estimation in large social networks." Social Networks 1: 91-101.

––––– (1971) Statistical Inference in Graphs. Stockholm, Sweden: Swedish Research Institute of National Defense.

FREEMAN, L. C. (1979) "Centrality in social networks. I. Conceptual clarification." Social Networks 1: 215-239.

––––– (1977) "A set of measures of centrality based on betweenness." Sociometry 40: 35-41.

GALASKIEWICZ, J. (1979) Systems of Community Interorganizational Exchange. Beverly Hills, CA: Sage.

––––– and S. WASSERMAN (1981) "A dynamic study of change in a regional corporate network." American Sociological Review 46: 475-484.

GOODMAN, L. A. (1961) "Snowball sampling." Annals of Mathematical Statistics 32: 148-170.

GOULD, P. and A. GATRELL (1980) "A structural analysis of a game: the Liverpool v Manchester united cup final of 1977." Social Networks 2: 253-274.

GRANOVETTER, M. (1977) "Reply to Morgan and Rytina." American Journal of Sociology 83: 727-729.

––––– (1976) "Network sampling: some first steps." American Journal of Sociology 81: 1287-1303.

––––– (1974) Getting a Job: A Study of Contacts and Careers. Cambridge, MA: Harvard University Press.

––––– (1973) "The strength of weak ties." American Journal of Sociology 78: 1360-1380.

HALLINAN, M. T. (1978) "The process of friendship formation." Social Networks 24: 193-210.

––––– (1974) The Structure of Positive Sentiment. Amsterdam: Elsevier.

HANSEN, K. L. (1981) "'Black' exchange and its system of social control," pp. 70-83 in David Willer and Bo Anderson (eds.) Networks, Exchange, and Coercion. New York: Elsevier-North Holland.

HARARY, F. (1969) Graph Theory. Reading, MA: Addison-Wesley.

––––– (1959) "On the measurement of structural balance." Behavioral Science 4: 316-323.

––––– R. NORMAN, and D. CARTWRIGHT (1965) Structural Models. New York: John Wiley.

HARARY, F. and I. C. ROSS (1957) "A procedure for clique detection using the group matrix." Sociometry 20: 205-215.

HARTIGAN, J. A. (1975) Clustering Algorithms. New York: John Wiley.

––––– and M. A. WONG (1979) "K-means clustering algorithm." Journal of the Royal Statistical Society C (Applied Statistics) 28: 100-108.

HEIDER, F. (1979) "On balance and attribution," pp. 11-23 in Paul W. Holland and Samuel Leinhardt (eds.) Perspectives on Social Network Research. New York: Academic.

––––– (1946) "Attitudes and cognitive organizations." Journal of Psychology 21: 107-112.

HEIL, G. and H. C. WHITE (1976) "An algorithm for finding simultaneous homo-morphic correspondences between graphs and their image graphs." Behavioral Science 21: 26-45.

HOLLAND, P. W. and S. LEINHARDT (1978) "An omnibus test for social structure using triads." Sociological Methods & Research 7: 227-256.

——— (1975) "Local structure in social networks," pp. 1-45 in D. R. Heise (ed.) Sociological Methodology 1976. San Francisco: Jossey-Bass.

——— (1970) "A method for detecting structure in sociometric data." American Journal of Sociology 76: 492-513.

HOMANS, G. (1950) The Human Group. New York: Harcourt, Brace, Jovanovich.

HUBBELL, C. H. (1965) "An input-output approach to clique identification." Sociometry 28: 377-399.

HUNTER, J. E. (1979) "Toward a general framework for dynamic theories of sentiment in small groups derived from theories of attitude change," pp. 223-238 in Paul W. Holland and Samuel Leinhardt (eds.) Perspectives on Social Network Research. New York: Academic.

JOHNSON, S. C. (1967) "Hierarchical clustering schemes." Psychometrika 32: 241-254.

JÖRESKOG, K. G. (1969) "A general approach to confirmatory maximum likelihood factor analysis." Psychometrika 34: 183-202.

KADUSHIN, C. (1968) "Power, influence, and social circles: A new methodology for studying opinion makers." American Sociological Review 33: 685-699.

——— (1966) "The friends and supporters of psychotherapy: on social circles in urban life." American Sociological Review 31: 786-802.

KANDEL, D. B. (1978) "Homophily, selection, and socialization in adolescent friendships." American Journal of Sociology 84: 427-436.

KAPFERER, B. (1969) "Norms and the manipulation of relationships in a work context," pp. 181-244 in J. Clyde Mitchell (ed.) Social Networks in Urban Situations. Manchester, England: Manchester University Press.

KILLWORTH, P. D. and H. R. BERNARD (1979) "Informant accuracy in social network data III. A comparison of triadic structure in behavioral and cognitive data." Social Networks 2: 19-46.

——— (1976) "Informant accuracy in social network data." Human Organization 35: 269-286.

KLOVDAHL, A. S. (1981) "A note on images of networks." Social Networks 3: 197-214.

KNOKE, D. (forthcoming) "Organization sponsorship and influence reputation of social influence associations." Social Forces.

——— (1981) "Commitment and detachment in voluntary associations." American Sociological Review 46: 141-158.

——— and R. S. BURT (1982) "Prominence," in Ronald S. Burt and Michael J. Minor (eds.) Applied Network Analysis: Structural Methodology for Empirical Social Research. Beverly Hills, CA: Sage.

KNOKE, D. and E. O. LAUMANN (1982) "The social organization of national policy domains," in Nan Lin and Peter V. Marsden (eds.) Social Structure and Network Analysis. Beverly Hills, CA: Sage.

KNOKE, D. and J. R. WOOD (1981) Organized for Action: Commitment in Voluntary Associations. New Brunswick, NJ: Rutgers University Press.

KRUSKAL, J. B. and M. WISH (1978) Multidimensional Scaling. Beverly Hills, CA: Sage.

LANKFORD, P. M. (1974) "Comparative analysis of clique identification methods." Sociometry 37: 287-305.

LAUMANN, E. O. (1973) Bonds of Pluralism. New York: John Wiley.

——— (1966) Prestige and Association in an Urban Community. Indianapolis: Bobbs-Merrill.

——— J. GALASKIEWICZ, and P. V. MARSDEN (1978) "Community structure as interorganizational linkages," pp. 455-484 in A. Inkeles et al. (eds.) Annual Review of Sociology, Vol. 4. Palo Alto, CA: Annual Reviews.

LAUMANN, E. O., P. V. MARSDEN, and J. GALASKIEWICZ (1977) "Community influence structures: Replication and extension of a network approach." American Journal of Sociology 85: 594-631.

LAUMANN, E. O., P V. MARSDEN, and D. PRENSKY (1982) "The boundary specification problem in network analysis," in R. S. Burt and M. J. Minor (eds.) Applied Network Analysis: Structural Methodology for Empirical Social Research. Beverly Hills, CA: Sage.

LAUMANN, E. O. and F. U. PAPPI (1976) Networks of Collective Action: A Perspective on Community Influence Systems. New York: Academic.

LAUMANN, E. O., L. M. VERBRUGGE, and F. U. PAPPI (1974) "A causal modelling approach to the study of a community elite's influence structure," in Edward O. Laumann and Franz U. Pappi, Networks of Collective Action. New York: Academic.

LAZARSFELD, P. F., B. R. BERELSON, and H. GAUDET (1948) The People's Choice: How the Voter Makes Up His Mind in a Presidential Campaign. New York: Columbia University Press.

LEAVITT, H. J. (1951) "Some effects of communication patterns on group performance." Journal of Abnormal Psychology 46: 38-50.

LEIK, R. K. and B. F. MEEKER (1975) Mathematical Sociology. Englewood Cliffs, NJ: Prentice-Hall.

LEIK, R. K. and R. NAGASAWA (1970) "A sociometric basis for measuring social status and social structure." Sociometry 33: 55-78.

LEINHARDT, S. (1972) "Developmental change in the sentiment and structure of children's groups." American Sociological Review 37: 202-212.

LEVINE, J. (1972) "The sphere of influence." American Sociological Review 37: 14-27.

LIN, N. (1976) Foundations of Social Research. New York: McGraw-Hill.

——— (1975) "Analysis of communication relations," in Gerhard J. Hanneman and William J. McElwen (eds.) Communication and Behavior. Reading, MA: Addison-Wesley.

——— P. W. DAYTON, and P. GREENWALD (1978) "Analyzing the instrumental use of relations in the context of social structure." Sociological Methods & Research 7: 149-166.

——— (1977) "The urban communication network and social stratification: a 'small world' experiment," pp. 107-119 in D. B. Ruben (ed.) Communication Yearbook, Vol. 1. New Brunswick, NJ: Transaction Books.

LINCOLN, J. R. and J. MILLER (1979) "Work and friendship ties in organizations: A comparative analysis of relational networks." Administrative Science Quarterly 24: 181-199.

LINDZEY, G. and E. F. BORGATTA (1954) "Sociometric measurement," pp. 405-448 in Gardner Lindzey (ed.) Handbook of Social Psychology, Vol. 1. Cambridge, MA: Addison-Wesley.

LINTON, R. (1936) The Study of Man. New York: Appleton-Century-Crofts.

LORRAIN, F. and H. C. WHITE (1971) "Structural equivalence of individuals in social networks." Journal of Mathematical Sociology 1: 49-80.

LUCE, R. D. (1950) "Connectivity and generalized cliques in sociometric group structure." Psychometrika 15: 169-190.

——— and A. PERRY (1949) "A method of matrix analysis of group structure." Psychometrika 14: 94-116.

McCALLISTER, L. and C. S. FISCHER (1978) "A procedure for surveying personal networks." Sociological Methods & Research 7: 131-148.

McCONAGHY, M. J. (1981) "The common role structure: improved blockmodeling methods applied to two communities' elites." Sociological Methods & Research 9: 267-285.

McFARLAND, D. and D. BROWN (1973) "Social distance as a metric: a systematic introduction to smallest space analysis," pp. 213-253 in Edward O. Laumann, Bonds of Pluralism: The Form and Substance of Urban Social Networks. New York: John Wiley.

MacQUEEN, J. (1967) "Some methods for classification and analysis of multivariate observations," pp. 281-297 in L. M. LeCan and J. Neyman (eds.) Proceedings of the Fifth Berkeley Symposium on Mathematical Statistics and Probability, Vol. 1. Berkeley: University of California Press.

McQUITTY, L. L. (1957) "Elementary linkage analysis for isolating orthogonal and oblique types and typal relevancies." Educational and Psychological Measurement 17: 207-229.

MacRAE, D., Jr. (1960) "Direct factor analysis of sociometric data." Sociometry 23: 360-371.

MANDEL, M. and C. WINSHIP (1981) "Roles and positions: an extension of the blockmodel approach." Northwestern University, Evanston, Illinois. (unpublished)

MARIOLIS, P. (1975) "Interlocking directorates and control of corporations." Social Science Quarterly 56: 425-439.

MARSHALL, J. F. (1971) "Topics and networks in intra-village communication," pp. 160-166 in Steven Polgar (ed.) Culture and Population: A Collection of Current Studies. Monograph 9. Chapel Hill, NC: Carolina Population Center.

MILGRAM, S. (1967) "The small world problem." Psychology Today 1: 61-67.

MILLER, J., J. R. LINCOLN, and J. OLSON (1981) "Rationality and equity in professional networks: gender and race as factors in the stratification of interorganizational systems." American Journal of Sociology 87: 308-335.

MITCHELL, J. C. (1969) "The concept and use of social networks," pp. 1-50 in J. Clyde Mitchell (ed.) Social Networks in Urban Situations. Manchester, England: Manchester University Press.

MORENO, J. L. (1934) Who Shall Survive? Foundations of Sociometry, Group Psychotherapy, and Sociodrama. Washington, DC: Nervous and Mental Disease Monograph 58.

MORGAN, D. L. and S. RYTINA (1977) "Comment on 'Network Sampling: some first steps' by Mark Granovetter." American Journal of Sociology 83: 722-727.

MORGAN, D. L. and L. S. WOLFARTH (1980) "Testing the goodness-of-fit of block-models." Indiana University. (mimeo)

MULHERIN, J. P., H. M. KAWABATA, and J. A. SONQUIST (1981) "Related data-bases for combined network and attribute data files: an SAS implementation." Connections 4: 22-31.

MULLINS, N., L. HARGENS, P. HECHT, and E. KICK (1977) "The group structure of cocitation clusters: a comparative study." American Sociological Review 42: 552-562.

NADEL, S. F. (1957) The Theory of Social Structure. London: Cohen & West.

PERRUCCI, R. and M. PILISUK (1970) "Leaders and ruling elites: the interorgani-zational bases of community power." American Sociological Review 35: 1040-1056.

Project in Structural Analysis (1981) STRUCTURE: a computer program providing basic data for the analysis of empirical positions in a system of actors. Computer Program 1. Berkeley: University of California, Survey Research Center.

PROCTOR, C. H. (1979) "Graph sampling compared to conventional sampling," pp. 301-318 in Paul W. Holland and Samuel Leinhardt (eds.) Perspectives on Social Network Research. New York: Academic.

RAPOPORT, A. and W. J. HOVARTH (1961) "A study of a large sociogram." Behav-ioral Science 6: 279-291.

ROGERS, E. M. and D. L. KINCAID (1981) Communication Networks: Toward a New Paradigm for Research. New York: Macmillan.

ROISTACHER, R. C. (1979) "Acquisition and management of social network data," pp. 471-487 in P. W. Holland and S. Leinhardt (eds.) Perspectives on Social Network Research. New York: Academic.

——— (1974) "A review of mathematical models in sociometry." Sociological Methods & Research 3: 123-171.

ROSKAM, E. and J. C. LINGOES (1970) "MINESSA-1: a FORTRAN program for the smallest space analysis of square symmetric matrices." Behavioral Science 15: 204-220.

RUNGER, G. and S. WASSERMAN (1980) "Longitudinal analysis of friendship net-works." Social Networks 2: 143-154.

SAILER, L. D. (1978) "Structural equivalence: meaning and definition, computation and application." Social Networks 1: 73-90.

SAMPSON, S. F. (1969) "Crisis in a cloister." Ph.D. dissertation, Cornell University, Ithaca, New York.

SCHWARTZ, J. E. (1977) "An examination of CONCOR and related methods for blocking sociometric data," pp. 255-282 in D. R. Heise (ed.) Sociological Method-ology 1977. San Francisco: Jossey-Bass.

SEIDMAN, S. B. and B. L. FOSTER (1978) "A graph-theoretic generalization of the clique concept." Journal of Mathematical Sociology 6: 139-154.

SHEINGOLD, C. A. (1973) "Social networks and voting: the resurrection of a research agenda." American Sociological Review 39: 712-720.

SNYDER, D. and E. L. KICK (1979) "Structural position in the world system and economic growth, 1955-1970: a multiple network analysis of transnational inter-actions." American Journal of Sociology 84: 1096-1126.

SONQUIST, J. (1980) "Concepts and tactics in analyzing social network data." Connec-tions 3: 33-56.

———— and T. KOENIG (1975) "Interlocking directorates in the top U.S. corporations: a graph theory approach." Insurgent Sociologist 5: 196-229.

TRAVERS, J. and S. MILGRAM (1969) "An experimental study of the small world problem." Sociometry 32: 425-443.

Van der GEER, J. P. (1971) Introduction to Multivariate Analysis for the Social Sciences. San Francisco: Freeman.

WASSERMAN, S. (1980) "Analyzing social networks as stochastic processes." Journal of the American Statistical Association 75: 280-294.

———— (1979) "A stochastic model for directed graphs with transition rates determined by reciprocity," pp. 392-412 in K. Schuessler (ed.) Sociological Methodology 1980. San Francisco: Jossey-Bass.

WHITE, D. R. and K. P. REITZ (1982) "Rethinking the role concept: social networks, homorphisms and equivalence of positions," in L. C. Freeman, A. K. Romney, and D. R. White (eds.) Research Methods and Social Network Analysis. Irvine: University of California, School of Social Sciences. (unpublished)

WHITE, H. C. (1977) "Probabilities of homomorphic mappings from multiple graphs." Journal of Mathematical Psychology 16: 121-134.

———— (1963) An Anatomy of Kinship. Englewood Cliffs, NJ: Prentice-Hall.

———— (1961) "Management conflict and sociometric structure." American Journal of Sociology 67: 185-187.

———— A. BOORMAN, and R. L. BREIGER (1976) "Social structure from multiple networks 1. Blockmodels of roles and positions." American Journal of Sociology 81: 730-780.

WILLIAMSON, O. E. (1970) Corporate Control and Business Behavior. Englewood Cliffs, NJ: Prentice-Hall.

WOOD, J. R. (1981) Leadership in Voluntary Organizations: The Controversy Over Social Action in Protestant Churches. New Brunswick, NJ: Rutgers University Press.

DAVID KNOKE is Professor of Sociology and Director, Institute of Social Research at Indiana University, where he specializes in research on political behavior. With Edward O. Laumann, he is studying the social organization of the national energy and health policy domains. His recent books are Log-linear Models *(coauthored with Peter J. Burke; Sage Publications),* Organized for Action *(with James R. Wood; Rutgers University Press); and* Statistics for Social Data Analysis *(with George W. Bohrnstedt; Peacock Publishers).*

JAMES H. KUKLINSKI is Associate Professor of Political Science at Indiana University. His research interests are in American politics and democratic theory.

Quantitative Applications in the Social Sciences

(a Sage University Papers Series)

$5.00 each

SAGE PUBLICATIONS, INC.
P.O. BOX 5024
BEVERLY HILLS, CALIFORNIA 90210

Place
Stamp
here